God's Love in Human Language

God's Love
in
Human Language

*A Study of the Meaning of Marriage
and Conjugal Responsibility*

Cornelius J. van der Poel, C.S.Sp.

DUQUESNE UNIVERSITY PRESS
1969

NIHIL OBSTAT

Thomas J. Green, J.C.D.
a.h.d.

IMPRIMATUR

✠ Walter W. Curtis, S.T.D.
Bishop of Bridgeport, Conn.

Contents

PREFACE

The words *totality* and *integrity* which appear frequently in this excellent presentation on marriage reflect the central thrust of Father van der Poel's thinking. His entire work is based upon the insight that marriage is a totality involving the entire human person.

His reflections on the significance of marriage in the Old and New Testaments set forth an integral vision of marriage both as a human and as a religious institution.

Married couples who have heard Father van der Poel's lectures have been deeply impressed by his presentation of marriage within the context of his basic insight into the totality of the human person. That same insight pervades the present volume, which is based upon Father van der Poel's lectures. Both married couples and those whose ministry it is to counsel married Christians will profit greatly from a deeper insight into the mystery and wonder that is marriage.

Not all will agree with Father van der Poel's interpretation of the encyclical HUMANAE VITAE. As one priest said after a lecture of Father van der Poel: "It is interesting—but is it what Pope Paul VI really said?" Inasmuch as these lectures were first given at a time when the encyclical was quite recent and very much in the mind of his listeners, an interpretation of the encyclical necessarily formed an integral part of Father van der Poel's discussion of marriage. As a moralist, he has engaged in some thinking out loud regarding the whole matter. He speaks and writes with great reverence for the teaching mission of the Church and the significance of the Holy Father's encyclical, both in regard to the development of Christian marital ethics and its application by conscientious couples to their immediate marital situation. While giving couples significant freedom in conscientious decision making, his emphasis upon their responsibility to accept the consequences of their decision makes it clear that he does not leave the door wide open to those who would disregard the teaching of the encyclical.

His book joins the ranks of many worthwhile, contemporary presentations of marriage for the inspiration and guidance of those who are married or about to be married as well as for those whose task it is to counsel married Christians.

WALTER W. CURTIS, S.T.D.
BISHOP OF BRIDGEPORT, CONN.

February 6, 1969

INTRODUCTION

"Why all these theoretical discussions? Why all these speculations? Why don't we just love one another? Love each other in marriage, love your family, love your neighbor! Doesn't Christ teach us in the Gospels that one who really loves God and his neighbor has fulfilled the whole law?" Such was the impatient comment of a mother of five young children during a study-group discussion on conjugal spirituality. There is so much truth in what she said.

It is almost fashionable today to write on marriage. It guarantees a rather wide circle of readers. In a host of books and articles one can find detailed studies on every aspect of marital love. Successful efforts have been made to trace the historical development of the present canonical form of the contract of marriage. Others deal with the rights and obligations of the partners. Special studies have been made about the psychological needs and personality fulfillment in conjugal life. The topic of divorce and indissolubility of marriage is popular, and above all the matter of birth regulation is perhaps the most interesting item in contemporary literature.

I am not trying to downgrade any of these important studies. One can only be grateful for the sincere in-

terest which exists everywhere for this segment of life.
It is so indispensable for human relationship with God.
However, I am afraid that in the vast multitude of
excellent treatises it becomes extremely difficult for the
everyday couple (granted that they have the time to
read them) to get a clear picture of what their human
love can and must mean in God's plan of creation and
redemption. But unfortunately the deep sacramental
meaning of marriage remains so easily a peripheral
aspect. The necessary occupation with the material
aspects of family life, the concern for one's own personality fulfillment, the education of the children, the
problems connected with the responsible limitation of
the family, these are only a few of the concerns which
constantly present themselves to the conscientious
couple. These needs and concerns ask so much of
their attention that there is hardly any time left to sit
down and reflect upon the basis of it all. The words of
St. Paul: "Husbands should love their wives just as
Christ loved the Church, and sacrificed Himself for her,
to make her holy" (Eph. 5:25), do not have their full
impact upon their married life.

Christ's love for the Church and the Church's response to Christ is a total giving of self. It is this total
and unreserved self-giving in every aspect of daily life,
which is in its deepest human reality the essence of
marriage and which also provides the basis for its profound sacramental meaning. The married life of the
couple in Christian understanding is at the same time
the sign and the reality of this sanctifying love of God
for his people. It is the responsibility and the greatness
of the married couple to make this sanctifying and
redeeming love of God visibly present in their own life
as husband and wife and as parents. To live this love

and to communicate this love to others is the commission which they have accepted before God, before the community of the Church and before all mankind.

It is the purpose of this book to speak about this human and sacramental reality. Problems related to Canon Law on marriage have been avoided, in order to concentrate exclusively upon this basic question: How can everyday married life become indeed the visible reality of God's love in human language?

This present work is based on a series of lectures given to the couples who work in the Pre-Cana and Cana Conferences in the Diocese of Bridgeport, Connecticut, and to other interested couples. I want to take this opportunity to express my sincere thanks to the Most Reverend Walter W. Curtis, Bishop of Bridgeport and Episcopal Chairman of the National Catholic Family Life Bureau, for his encouragement in this specific work. I also want to give the assurance of my deep gratitude to the Director of the Family Life Bureau in Bridgeport and to his assistants and to the many others whose invaluable cooperation has made this work possible.

All scriptural quotations have been taken from the Confraternity version, 1961 edition.

CORNELIUS J. VAN DER POEL, C.S.Sp.

Chapter One

THE SACRAMENT OF MARRIAGE

In the very expression "the sacrament of marriage" we combine two aspects of one concept. We speak about "marriage in itself" and this means marriage as an institution of creation which belongs to humanity as such, and, secondly, we refer to marriage as a sacrament, and this means a manifestation of the redemptive action of Christ, made visible in the human reality of marriage. These two aspects are not two separate realities which can exist independently, but are rather one and the same reality, which is fully human, and has become a visible manifestation of the communication of God's redemptive grace through Christ. For those who believe in Christ and who are members of the visible presence of Christ, which is the Church, marriage and sacrament coincide.

However, for the proper understanding of what the sacrament of marriage is we need to consider these two aspects separately, i.e., "marriage as earthly reality" and "marriage as a sign of the communication of grace." Our purpose is not to treat them as distinct realities, but to come by way of a proper understanding of each aspect to a better understanding of the totality.

1. The General Meaning of a Sacrament

Before we can approach the subject of the sacrament of marriage, it is necessary to have first an accurate understanding of what we mean by the word "sacrament."

A sacrament has usually been defined as an outwardly perceptible sign, instituted by Christ, by which grace is signified and given to men. However correct this definition might be, it harbors a danger of being misunderstood. It is so easy to see a sacrament as a *thing,* or as a liturgical action or performance, the occasion on which God gives graces to the receiver who is well disposed. If we put it this way, there is a real possibility that we will miss the deeper reality and meaning of a sacrament, because a sacrament itself is not just a thing, but in its deepest reality it is a salvific action of Christ Himself, or *a divine bestowal of grace in* an outwardly perceptible form which makes the bestowal manifest.[1]

To understand this definition correctly we must go back to the life of Christ on earth. Christ is the God-Man, the second person of the Blessed Trinity, who assumed human nature, lived a human

[1] E. Schillebeecks, *Christ the Sacrament of the Encounter With God,* Sheed and Ward, New York, 1963, p. 15.

life, died upon the cross and arose from the dead. But the life of Jesus was not merely a life that was lived at a certain moment in human history. It was the fulfillment of a mission, namely, the salvation and sanctification of mankind. Man was in need of this salvation because from its very beginning mankind did not respond to the invitation which God the Creator had given to it.

As far as human knowledge, aided by revelation can know, God had destined man to live in an intimate friendship with Him, to share and participate in His divine life in eternity. But man has received the task to live this life in an earthly fashion before his eternal union in the glory of God. It was the personal responsibility of man to respond to this invitation by making his earthly life in a very true sense the image and likeness of God.

Unfortunately, man did not respond to this invitation. Instead of making his human reality a true expression of God's image and likeness, he concentrated upon himself, searching for his own, independent value and disregarding the orientation to God which would have made him on earth the visible manifestation of God's life and love. But despite this lack of response by man, the divine calling and the destiny to participate in the life of God remained, though it was hidden and largely overrun by human self-centeredness.

It is here that the mission of Christ finds its place. Where man failed to respond to the invitation of God, God himself assumed human nature. In the second person of the Blessed Trinity He assumed flesh and blood and He became man. He lived a human life in history together with other human beings. He shared in all the needs and desires of humanity. He underwent all the struggles, the hardships and difficulties which are proper to man. In brief, in everything He was found equal to man except in sin. Where humanity from its origin had failed to respond in a suitable way to the Creator, this same humanity now gave a suitable response to God in the Person of Christ. The life, the teaching, the work, the suffering and the death of Christ were one constant and total self-giving of man to God, "I have come from heaven, not to do my own will, but the will of him who sent me" (Jn 6:38). In Christ the Father offers again to humanity the invitation for a life of the most intimate union with God. The task of Christ was then to "expound what was hidden from the beginning of the world," namely, "the mystery of God with us."

In His human life Jesus was God. But God in His divine reality is beyond the reach of human perception. In Christ God reached out to men and made Himself visible to them. Christ was at the same time the reality of God and the sign under which this divine reality was made visible to men. Christ was the sacrament of God. He was not God hiding behind a human face, but God manifesting Himself in humanity. The actions which Christ performed were human actions but, at the same time, they were actions of God, who communicated His life to mankind and invited all men to accept it. Christ's action was the communication of divine life to humanity, but at the same time it was the action of men who in Christ respond to God's invitation, who in Christ accept this invitation. Thus the actions of Christ were in the very true sense "redemptive actions." They, too, were the sign and reality of the grace-giving, the sanctifying action of God.

This visible sanctifying action of Christ came to an end in His death upon the cross, but His mission to humanity did not cease with His death. He established His Church, not just as an organization in which He could continue His preaching, but as the visible expression and continuation of His mission, namely, the communication of this participation in divine life to every man who believes in Jesus and accepts this vocation of man— a vocation which was "hidden since the foundation of the world" (Mt. 13:35) and which was expounded by Jesus, and which still is continued by Jesus. He Himself is glorified and is therefore beyond the reach of human perception, but His salvific action is performed and made visible in and through the actions of the Church.

The total life and action of the human being who orients himself to God can in a certain way be called sacramental, but there are specific actions in which the acceptance and following of Christ is made visible in a special way in and through the Church as the visible presence of Christ. Such specific actions we call in technical terms "the sacraments of the Church." It is not just a ceremony on the occasion of which God gives graces. It is the visible redemptive and sanctifying action of Christ, performed in and through the visible Church. It is truly the action of Christ in which salvation is bestowed. One of these actions is the sacrament of marriage.

2. Marriage as an Earthly Reality

Let us first look at marriage as it exists in humanity. Here we see marriage as the result of a social structure. Abstractly man can exist and be entirely human without being married, but the structure of marriage is so intimately connected with human life and existence that we might see it as a necessary element in humanity. As the relationship between two human beings, marriage is necessarily most intimately connected with the social and cultural pattern of the group in which it exists. The history of mankind, as far as it can be traced back to its origin, gives a variety of such social patterns in which marriage was lived. According to the cultural pattern, marriage had a different structure and imposed upon the partners different responsibilities.

We find indications of different marital structures in the Bible. When we read the creation narratives we see that God created Eve from a rib

of Adam and "He brought her to man" (Gen.
2:23). A little later we read that the woman "will
yearn for her husband, yet he will lord over her"
(3:16). It does not require much imagination to
recognize here the basic structure of a patriarchal
society in which the woman leaves her own family
and enters into the family of the husband. On the
other hand, we see in Genesis 2:24 "This is why a
man leaves his father and mother and joins to his
wife." It is easy to read in this sentence the basic
structure of matriarchal society in which the man
leaves his family and becomes a member of the
family of his wife. His children are born into her
family and receive her name.

To find this ambiguity in the beginning of the
Book of Genesis need not surprise us, since we
have here a collection of pre-biblical traditions
which tell us how ancient times understood the
origin of the world and of humanity. The message of Genesis is that God is the origin of everything. So also both family structures can be seen
as acceptable before God.

In other circumstances of historical development we see what we might call "the extended
family." This is the familial (and social) structure
in which three or more generations live close together and work together for the development of
the same family enterprise. It was a common condition in earlier rural society. In its life situation
and its working conditions the family formed one
unit under one common authority, which often

seemed semi-patriarchal. These three stages of development in family structure, though very different in many aspects, had some basic elements in common. In all of them marriage removed one's individual status since the new wife or husband became in a very real sense a member of the family unit.

Moreover, the new member of the family was to take part in the development of the family property, not only by contributing to the birth of new life into the family, but also by personal contributions of economic importance, such as the ability to join in the work of the family. This had as a consequence that in the arrangement for the marriage the judgment of the family as a whole concerning the qualities of the prospective new wife or husband was very important.

Notice also that family life itself, had a very peculiar structure. Husband and wife worked not only side by side but also with many other members of the family. Many tensions which might arise between the marriage partners could find an outlet within the larger family group. We might say that when these structures existed marriage and family life in many respects had their origin and their stability in elements which lay outside the interpersonal relationship of the married couple itself.

Another additional factor was that the children who were born into the family were considered as a financial asset, as so many more hands to expand and to improve the family estate. Also for the children themselves, their future was largely determined for them by those who were the leaders of the family group. The young did not, as a rule, leave to build up their own life and future; moreover, it was not rare that not all the men in the family would be permitted to marry, especially in cases where the family estate could not provide for more than a certain number of persons.

These conditions have greatly changed since the industrial revolution. The rural setting has changed to city dwelling. The future became a personal venture; the family unit began to differ greatly from its former group formation. The choice of a marriage partner became a personal matter in the full sense of the word, and the qualities required in the partner were based more on personality than on the ability to work. The stability of marriage had to find its sources within the marital structure itself and within the interpersonal relationship of the partners. In the growing demand for education and social progress, the children became a liability rather than an asset. This is to a large extent the situation in which we live today.

It seems obvious that within the different marital structures the responsibility of the partners to each other, to their children, and to society is also different. It would be incorrect to try to make a judgment as to which form would be the better one. Each form of marriage can be used in accordance with the law of God, but it can also be lived contrary to God's law. Perhaps we could say that, as a rule, the present form places higher demands on personal development and on personal responsibility, and that therefore it can offer a better possibility for a more profound commitment of the spouses to each other and to God. However, the important point is that we see that marriage itself is an earthly reality which is expressed in a variety of ways. This emphasizes that the deeper meaning and goal of marriage goes beyond the external structure.

We must now search for the meaning of marriage as a most intimate union of two human beings, a union of love which is lasting and which imposes upon each of them responsibilities toward each other and toward God. The search for the meaning of this inter-human relationship and this relationship to God should start in the Scriptures.

A. *Marriage in the Old Testament*

In the first part of the Book of Genesis we read the creation narratives. There are two such narratives in Genesis. The oldest one is Chapter 2:18–25. The second one which was written approximately 600 years later, is Chapter 1: 27–28. Both deal essentially with the same subject, the creation of man by God. Both narratives are "historical," not in the sense of giving account of the actual happenings, but insofar as they bring us the message that at the beginning of human history man was created by God. The oldest narrative says:

> The Lord God said: It is not good that man is alone; I will make him a helper like himself. When the Lord had formed out of the ground all the beasts of the field and the birds of the air, he brought them to the man to see what he would call them; for that which the man called each of them would be its name. The man called all the cattle, all the birds of the air and all the beasts of the field; but he found no helper like himself.

> The Lord God cast man into a deep sleep and, while he slept, took one of his ribs and closed up its place with flesh. And the rib which the Lord God took from man, he made into a woman and brought her to him. Then the man said: "She now is bone of my bone and flesh of my flesh; she shall be called woman, for from man she has been taken."

Then the author of this account closes his story with the words: "For this reason a man leaves his father and mother and clings to his wife, and the two shall become one flesh."

The second narrative is much shorter:

> God created man in his image. In the image of God he created him. Male and female he created them. Then God blessed them and said to them: "Be fruitful and multiply; fill the earth and subdue it. Have dominion over the fish of the

sea, the birds of the air, the cattle and all the animals that crawl on the earth."

There is no need to go into a detailed exegesis of these texts. For our purpose it is sufficient to indicate a few of the most important points of the message which the Scriptures want to convey to us.

1. Being man and being woman, that is, the differentiation of sexes, is a gift of God to humanity. If mankind has a task to fulfill on earth, then it will be as man or as woman and in cooperation of the sexes.

2. Man and woman have been given to each other in marriage by God: ". . . and He brought her to him." This statement is made in the Scriptures about the beginning of mankind, and it means, in the style of the ancient writers, that this belonging to each other is of divine origin. So marriage itself is a gift of God to humanity, and the mutual closeness—". . . and he shall cling to his wife"—is part of this gift of God to man.

3. Man and woman are together for mutual cooperation as Yahweh says: "I will make him an helper like himself." The word "helper" does not indicate a role of subservience. In the Scriptures Yahweh himself is often referred to as "the helper" of Israel. Elsewhere in the Scriptures the wife is called "a steadying column" for the husband (Sir. 36:24). It rather indicates that man

and woman are equal in dignity because she was taken from a rib of Adam, and he called her: "bone of my bone and flesh of my flesh." This already tells us how much they belong together, and how much their task must be one.

4. The task which they have to fulfill is really one since the two must "become one flesh." The expression "to become one flesh" does not primarily refer to sexual relationship, but rather to the fact that they together must become one source and principle of operation. This is indicated in the sentence: "For this reason shall the man leave his father and mother and cling to his wife." In the biblical language to leave one's father and mother means to go out on a mission on which one has been sent. Though one has been sent on his mission and has his task outlined to a large extent, still one retains one's own responsibility for the task. This task is to become the one flesh, the source from which the new family originates but also the source by which nature is changed into culture: "Be fruitful and multiply and subdue the earth."

The task of marriage which the creation narrative assigns to men is a comprehensive, all-encompassing task. It includes, as in one indivisible unity, the various aspects of procreation as well as cultural and social development.

This picture of totality must be kept in mind because it is this total view of marriage as the procreative and the cultural source of humanity which is taken in the Scriptures as the vehicle to transmit to mankind the meaning and the reality of God's covenant with his people. The first time this matter comes up is in the Book of Osee. The prophet does not at all intend to give any specific theology on marriage. His sole purpose is to explain the relationship between God and His people, but to explain this relationship he uses marriage, and in doing so he teaches indirectly something about marriage as well.

At the time of the prophet Osee, Israel had abandoned the religion of Yahweh and almost all of the people joined in the worship of Baal. Marital fidelity was disregarded and the women participated in fertility rites, giving themselves to temple prostitution, a form of worship in which fertility was asked from the god Baal by having sexual relations with such "dedicated" women. Yahweh commanded Osee to take Gomer, a temple prostitute, as his wife and to have children with her. Three children were born in this marriage. The reason why Yahweh commanded this marriage was that "the country itself has become nothing but a whore by abandoning Yahweh" (Osee, 1:2). After a short time, Gomer became unfaithful to Osee and was taken in marriage by another man. Yahweh commanded Osee to take her back, pay the price which her present husband asked and love her again, "Go a second time, give your love to a woman, beloved by her husband but an adultress in spite of it, just as Yahweh gives his love to the sons of Israel though they turn to other gods . . ." (Osee, 3:1).

The message of the prophet is clear.

1. Yahweh wanted to convey to Israel the evil of abandoning the religion of Yahweh. He made this visible in the unfaithfulness of Gomer.

2. He wanted to show how strong and unbreakable His love was for Israel. He manifested this in the person of Osee who took the unfaithful wife back and payed the price which her husband demanded.

3. Finally, Yahweh wanted to make clear how infinite His mercy was for the sinners, and this He showed by the love which Osee gave to the unfaithful woman.

The whole prophecy is focused upon the covenant between Yahweh and Israel, but Osee's marriage becomes the living human expression of the evil of unfaithfulness to Yahweh, and of Yahweh's endless love and mercy.

Osee's marriage is often used in prophetic writings to explain the relationship between Yahweh and his people. In Osee it was this one individual marriage which was used in this explanation; later in the Old Testament we see how infidelity to Yahweh was often referred to as "adultery." Perhaps the clearest description is found in the prophet Ezechiel. He describes (in Chapter 16) how Yahweh found Jerusalem as a little girl, abandoned, unwashed; how he took care of her and later contracted a marriage with her, but how she became unfaithful to Yahweh. Here the covenant relationship is directly expressed in terms of marriage, and unfaithfulness to the covenant is comparable to unfaithfulness in marriage. Later, in Chapter 26:48, Yahweh explicitly draws attention to the punishment which the country will receive for its infidelity as he says: "I mean to purge the land of debauchery; all the women will thus be warned, and ape your debauchery no more." Just as the covenant relationship between Yahweh and his people is expressed in terms of marriage, so also is marital fidelity compared with the fidelity of God to His people.

In other prophets there is a progressive development in the use of marriage to explain the God-people relationship, the concern and the love of God, as well as the response which is expected from the people. We do not need to go into further detail. For our purpose here it suffices if we see that the total structure of marriage as a common task of the couple in mutual fidelity and love, is the human image of the relationship of love between God and his people. This was the concept of marriage that existed at the time of Jesus, and when He speaks and teaches about marriage it is against the background of the whole of the Old Testament.

B. *Marriage in the New Testament*

Nowhere in the New Testament did Christ give any sort of treatise that might be considered as a theology of marriage. In fact, He spoke very little about marriage itself. He accepted it as it existed. But still, on a number of occasions, He indicated that its meaning went beyond the external structure. The Kingdom of Heaven is compared with a banquet which a father gave in honor of the wedding of his son. The intimate joy and pure love of the young couple was an occasion to describe the joys of eternal union with God. He was present at the Wedding of Cana, which is significant as the presence of God at this union in love between man and woman. He even signified the special blessing which it has in the eyes of God, by performing for them a miracle. He gave the most important instruction, however, concerning marriage in answer to a question of the pharisees about the possibility of divorce and about the reason which may lead to it. In this answer He projected marriage back to its origin.

> Have you not read that the Creator from the beginning made them male and female, and said: "For this cause a man shall leave his father and mother and cleave to his wife, and the two shall become one flesh?" Therefore now they are no longer two but one flesh. What therefore God has joined together let no man put asunder.
>
> (Mt. 19: 4–6).

Christ accepted marriage in its totality as it had been transmitted throughout the Old Testament, as this one principle and unity of operation and as the foundation for the continuation of humanity in all its various aspects. He lays special stress on its original indissolubility and presents it as an institution of a special divine design and value.

This special divine value which He attributes to it becomes clearer still in the further development of His conversation with the apostles. He explains to them that some people do not marry because they are born that way, others because they have been made so by men, others again do not marry for the sake of the kingdom of God. By this He indicates that marriage is a gift of God to mankind; it should not keep people away from God. Those who do not marry for the sake of the kingdom of God make manifest in their personal life of dedication to God the same reality which in another manner must be present also in married life, namely, that human life finds its fulfillment in an orientation to God.

This becomes more explicitly evident in the teaching of St. Paul, especially in Eph. 5:21–33:

> Be subject to one another in the fear of Christ. Let wives be subject to their husbands as to the Lord; because the husband is the head of the wife just as Christ is the head of the Church, being Himself savior of the body. But just as the Church is subject to Christ, so also let wives be to their

husbands in all things. Husbands love your wives just as Christ also loved the Church, and delivered Himself up for her, that He might sanctify her, cleansing her in the bath of water by means of the word; in order that He might present to Himself the Church in all her glory, not having a spot or wrinkle or any such thing, but that she might be holy and without blemish. Even thus ought husbands also to love their wives as their own bodies. He who loves his own wife loves himself. For no one ever hated his own flesh; on the contrary, he nourishes and cherishes it, as Christ also does the Church (because we are members of His body, made from His flesh and from His bones).

For this cause a man shall leave his father and mother and cleave to his wife; and the two shall become one flesh. This mystery is great—I mean in reference to Christ and the Church. However, let each one of you also love his wife just as he loves himself; and let the wife respect her husband.

In this text of St. Paul the explanation of the covenant of salvation and the understanding of marriage fuse into a unity. He describes how much Christ loves the Church, how much Christ has done for the Church. He delivered Himself up for her, He sacrificed Himself for her in order to sanctify her and make her beautiful. The description of St. Paul sounds as if it is inspired by what is written in Ezechiel, Chapter 16. This total love of

Christ for the Church must be the example of the true and sacrificial love between husband and wife. They must love each other as their own body.

Paul goes on to stress the oneness between the couple by pointing to the creation of mankind where God made them male and female, and "for this reason a man shall leave his father and mother and cling to his wife and the two shall become one flesh." This specific unity of husband and wife in so far as they are one principle of operation in sanctifying love, he calls "a great mystery" in reference to Christ and the Church. This is understood to mean that they express in human life and language in a visible and perceptible way the redeeming and sanctifying love which exists between Christ and the Church, that is, between Christ and the people who actually believe in Him.

So we see in the Scriptures as one line of progressive development and revelation that the creation of man as male and female is the earthly representation of God's creative love: He places in their hands the procreation of mankind and man's self-development in cultural expression. But the unity of man and woman goes beyond this. It becomes the sign by which the covenant between God and his people, i.e., the loving care of God for His people, is made known to man. Finally, in the fullness of revelation in the New Testament it has been made clear to man that this unity of marriage is the living human expression of Christ's salvific action, His sanctifying love for those who believe in Him.

3. Marriage as a Sacrament

From the foregoing we should now be able to see what the meaning is of marriage precisely *as a sacrament*. A sacrament is "Christ making His redemptive and sanctifying action visible in and through the ministry of the Church, which is the People of God." The Church as the people of God, in the strict sense of the word, are those who by a visible action have manifested their will to belong to this visible expression of the presence of the glorified Christ on earth. This means, by their baptism they have become part of this visible reality of Christ's presence on earth. When, then, man and woman who do express in their personal life Christ's sanctifying presence on earth by believing in Him and responding to Him, come together in a mutual self-giving which is total and unreserved and which comes forth from their love for each other, then this self-giving in love becomes the visible expression of the unreserved self-giving of Christ for the sanctification of the world and of the human response which mankind gives to Christ. This human response is total fidelity to Christ and thus sanctifying for those who give it. So also in marriage, the self-giving of the one to the other in total and mutual response shares in this same totality.

Accordingly, marriage remains what it was—an earthly reality, an institute of creation. But this same reality has become in and through Christ, in the strict sense of the word, a mystery of salvation.

There is no need to go into a detailed study of the development of Christian understanding of marriage throughout the centuries of history. It is sufficient for our purpose to know that although this sacrament of marriage concerns first of all the partners of the marriage itself, it is nonetheless a matter which concerns also human society at large, because no one can live without being a member of this human family. But it concerns also the Church at large because in and through the spouses the Church itself performs this salvific action of Christ. It stands to reason therefore that marriage must have some form of public expression in which this action becomes indeed an action of the Church as a whole. It stands to reason also that the authorities of the Church, who in a special way make the authority of Christ visible on earth, can make certain demands concerning the validity of marriage. However important all these aspects are, they should never obscure the exalted reality that marriage is in a very real sense, *The Love of God in Human Language*.

Chapter Two

LOVE, THE FOCAL POINT
OF MARRIAGE

When we considered marriage in the context of the creation narratives, we saw it as the mutual attraction and the cooperation between male and female which led them to an association of life in which they together became one principle and source of activity. This activity had as its purpose the mutual fulfillment of each partner, the development of culture, and above all the continuation of the human race. The various elements of this human institution are so intimately interwoven that the one cannot exist or prosper without the other, but at the same time the various aspects of this mission are impossible to realize unless the individual partners have the courage to see beyond their own individual interests and show a concern for each other. They know by experience that the other's welfare is one's own welfare, and that concentration on self-satisfaction holds the seed of destruction of their association and imperils the success of their mission.

It is especially under this aspect that marriage provides an earthly example illustrating the covenant between God and humanity. God's self-expression in created existence, in which God had given to man the response-ability to shape his own life in such a fashion that he would be in a special and real way the image and likeness of God, demands a continuous self-giving of God, but also a continual and faithful response on the part of man, in order that man might indeed unfold himself into the human representation of God's self-manifestation. Marriage cannot exist in its total reality without a mutual dedication of the spouses, nor can it be the human realization of God's caring love and concern without this same dedication.

St. Paul saw in marriage the great mystery of the Christ-Church relationship which is redemptive and sanctifying by its nature; hence the relationship of marriage cannot be real unless there is the same dedication of the one to the other as there is in the redemptive action of Christ and the response of the Church. Whichever way we look at marriage, its force and its focus always bear upon a quality which in human terms we call love.

Not without reason does Vatican Council II strongly emphasize that the Christian spouses precisely "in fulfilling their responsibilities of marriage and family will gradually come to their own self-fulfillment and to mutual sanctification, and precisely because of this they will come together to the glorification of God. But they should not

forget that their mutual sanctification unfolds itself gradually in the contents of their everyday life
in the mutuality of their christian conjugal love." [1]

1. The Meaning of Love

There is perhaps no other word in the human
vocabulary which is so often misused and so often
misinterpreted as is "love." The reason for this is
that there is perhaps no other term which tries to
comprehend so many human aspects and human
realities in a single word. "Love" is not a word
which indicates a certain thing or a certain condition in human life, but it rather tries to express in
one word the totality of relationships of one person to another and of the one person to his total
environment. Many persons of various professions
and levels of education and learning have tried to
give a definition or at least a description of the
word "love." Among the many possibilities I
choose this one:

> Love is the attitude of a human being in which
> he gives a proper value-response to another per-
> son. This value-response is not given for the sake
> of self-satisfaction or self-gratification, but for
> the good of the other. It is this unselfish re-
> sponse to a value in the other which constitutes
> the perfection and the fulfillment of the giver.[2]

[1] L. Janssens, *Echtelijke Liefde en Verantwoord Ouderschap,* De Vroente/Kasterlee, 1967, pp. 127–128.
[2] This descriptive definition is mainly based upon Dietrich
von Hildebrand, *Man and Woman,* Franciscan Herald Press,
1965, pp. 32 ff.

There are at least four distinct elements contained
in this:
   a) There is a relationship between two persons;
   b) The one recognizes values in the other and
      he responds to these values;
   c) This response is not for his own gratifica-
      tion, but it rather is an effort to make the
      other more complete;
   d) By doing so the giver reaches his own per-
      fection and fulfillment.

If this description of love contains any truth, we
can see in it the core of human existence, namely,
that the human being must develop himself and
grow to maturity, and this happens exactly
through his self-communication to others. Love is
something which places its mark on the whole of
human existence. It includes the whole of human
behavior. Let us listen for a moment to St. Paul:

> Charity is patient, is kind;
> Charity does not envy, is not pretentious, is not
>   puffed up;
> is not ambitious, is not self seeking, is not pro-
>   voked;
> thinks no evil, does not rejoice over wickedness,
> but rejoices with the truth;
> bears with all things, believes all things,
> hopes all things, endures all things (1 Cor. 13:
>   4–7).

It is hardly possible to give in such a compact
form a more complete list of interhuman relationships, and all of them are brought under one com-

mon denominator, or rather all of them stem from
one common source, and this source is called love.
What all these various qualities have in common is
that they are all directed to the other person, not
as an external performance, but as the deepest and
innermost giving of self as a person, so much that
St. Paul says: "And if I distribute all my goods to
feed the poor, and if I deliver my body to be
burned, yet do not have charity, it profits me nothing" (1 Cor. 13:3). This contains another element, namely, that if the giving of all my goods,
even for the sake of others, does not contain at the
same time the deepest giving of my personal self,
then all this giving does not make me a better
human being, because it would only be the outside
of my self, not the inner reality. Only when my
innermost self goes out to the other is it possible to
enrich myself.

It is no exaggeration to see here the true image
and likeness of God who does not gain by creation
and by human response, but whose glory is manifested in the simple and total giving of self to
others and for others. It may seem as if we have
passed from a consideration of human love to the
love of God, or to religious aspects of love. This is
not our intention at this moment; we simply want
to see the human reality of love. Let us look,
therefore, at the description of love as given by a
person who does not believe in Christ:

> Love is an active power in man; a power which
> breaks through the walls which separates man

from his fellowmen, which unites him with others;
love makes him overcome the sense of isolation
and separateness, yet permits him to be himself,
to retain his integrity. In love the paradox occurs
that two beings become one and yet remain two.[3]

This growth into a one-ness of two persons, of
which this description speaks, makes it clear that
the beloved person can never be degraded to an
"object," but the other is always seen as the equal
and even more than the equal because the lover
recognizes that the other deserves his self-giving.
The lover, without knowing by what power he is
driven, accepts the fact that his own life is empty
unless he can fill the life of the other with his, and
only then can he experience that in the fulfillment
of the other's life his own fulfillment will be ac-
complished. This demands a number of plain
human qualities, which are so intimately interwoven that the one cannot exist without the other.
Among the most important of them we could list
the following.

a) *Care*. This is the active power and the active concern which the human being has for something or for someone other than himself. Care
contains in reality two different things. It is a need
in ourselves in which we express the creative element which is so much part of our nature. We
realize that for our own existence we need to

[3] Erich Fromm, *The Art of Loving*, Bantam Books, 1963,
p. 17.

work, we must create and shape our own existence; it is our internal and innermost need which tells us that we are not self-sufficient, that if we want to take care of ourselves we have to go outside ourselves, whether it be to things and/or to persons. By doing so, we recognize at the same time that the other often does not attain completeness and fulfillment if we do not take care of it. This insight that the other is in need of us brings us to another element.

b) *Responsibility*. Responsibility is particularly a human quality. It is not in the first place a matter of a duty which was imposed from the outside. As man has been created by God, he received from the Creator a "response-ability" and, together with it, the unconscious urge to use this ability to respond, and the knowledge that by not using it he could never be the total being which he is able to be. This "response-ability" supposes in man also the ability to sense the needs to which he can give a response, to which he can direct his ability to respond. This combination creates in the inner reality of man what we now call "responsibility." He feels consciously or unconsciously that he can become himself to the fullness of his capacities only by responding to the expressed or unexpressed needs of the other. In his task of self-realization he recognizes that the realization and/or activation of the other is part of himself. His brother's life is part of his own life.

In the ancient oriental tradition incorporated in the Bible, which for us contains the word of God, and which is in reality the wisdom and understanding of the total human reality, this concept is brought very clearly to our attention in the story of Cain and Abel. After Cain had killed his brother and fled from Yahweh (i.e., he fled from his own conscience) Yahweh's word to him was not the question "Why did you kill your brother?" but "Where is your brother?" And Cain's answer was not that his brother was dead on the field, but his answer was a counter question: "Am I my brother's guardian?" In reference to this Bible story I would like to stress that

1) Cain heard in the depth of his conscience, that is, in the core of his own being, the cry of need of his brother, his fellowman. He did not feel total and complete without his fellowman.

2) At the same time he denied this need by asking: "Am I my brother's guardian?"

The self-imposed isolation of the human being, contrary to his own inner urge, is the ugliest sinfulness in man. His self-sufficiency becomes self-worship or idolatry. It is here that the full horror of Cain's sin was expressed: the isolation of the individual and the denial of his responsibility for the other. But concern and responsibility for the other can easily deteriorate into a harsh domination over the other and into using the other as an object for one's own gratification. How often does it not happen that so-called human concern for the other is nothing but a response to the compulsive needs of the individual to make himself feel important and indispensable? It is often self-seeking rather than openness for the needs of the other. It is here that attention must be drawn to another element, viz, respect.

c) *Respect.* It is necessary to have esteem for the other exactly as the other is. Respect is to see the other as a person with a unique individuality which is as sacred as our own individuality. It is to accept that the other has the same right and need to grow and develop as we have; and not only to accept that the other has a right to this development but also that in the full growth of the other our self-giving and the value of our own person achieve a level which otherwise cannot be attained.

It is in this respect for the other that the human being feels that he is becoming more human, because here he can in the most complete sense of the word go beyond himself and step out of his isolation. Here he exercises his freedom and here he experiences that he has made his own choice; his action for the unfolding of the other is not inspired by the blind instinct of self-preservation or self-gratification. He is not driven by an irrational urge, but he is human, he is free.

d) *Knowledge.* But respect for the other is impossible without knowledge. One can never respect what one does not know, because respect presupposes looking at the other and recognizing him as another person. Without knowledge, care and responsibility would be blind forces and instinctive urges. Knowledge enables us to make a free choice and to determine our direction. It makes our dedication to the other person a real self-giving. But it also increases the respect which we have for the other because it makes us realize that the depth of the other is as unfathomable as the depth of our own personality. It teaches us respect for his unique individuality. Thus it increases our love.

In this interplay of knowledge and respect, of care, concern and responsibility, love is never a static reality, but it is always a constant alertness and a being attuned to the needs of the other. It is always developing, it finds always new aspects and new expressions because the circumstances of life change from moment to moment. It is an answer to ups and downs, to joys and sorrows, because it is a response to the human life-situation. But within the total life-situation the expression of love is in its deepest foundation a mutual communication and exchange of life. We might say that:

> To love means to see what change is needed and to be willing to adapt oneself; it also means to be aware of the need for growth, and therefore love is a growing thing. Love is a feeling for the constantly changing circumstances in

which we live, and therefore love is a constant renewal.[4]

It is for this reason that love is always new and always exciting. When the expression of love becomes dull and monotonous, this means that one is not acutely aware of the present condition and need of the other person.

2. The Meaning of Christian Love

After spending so much time on an analysis of the meaning of human love, it may sound a little arrogant and perhaps prejudiced to ask, as a separate question, about the meaning of Christian love. It would seem to imply that human love is not Christian. This is not the case. The mission of Christ was to bring human love and human existence to its fulfillment, that is, to reveal the deepest meaning of human love. Shortly before His Passion Christ said: "A new commandment I give to you, that you love one another." Not as if love between men were not possible before, or as if it were not required before, but, as He explained the meaning of His commandment, "that as I have loved you, you also love one another" (Jn 13:34).

What was new in Christ's commandment was that the human love as it existed, as it was known and as it was practiced by men, was to become the

[4] C. J. Trimbos, *Healthy Attitudes Towards Love and Sex*, P. J. Kenedy & Sons, New York, 1964, p. 116.

visible expression of the God-man relationship. The qualities which existed in the divine love for humanity were to be made visible and approachable in the love between human beings, so that in this human expression the presence of God with men would become perceptible. "By this will all men know that you are my disciples, if you have love for one another" (Jn. 13:35)

If, then, we take into account that the disciples of Jesus were people who not only accepted a certain form of doctrinal statements which Jesus preached, but also and primarily people who had become partakers in His divine life, then we see that the fullness of human love was reached in the message of Christ to man: He brought the fullness of man's vocation to be the image and likeness of God.

What the quality was of His own love for humanity Christ expressed in the words, "as the Father has loved me so I have loved you" (Jn 15:9). But the love between the Father and the Son is the total and life-giving self-communication which exists in the eternal and invisible God. This same total and life-giving self-communication takes place between Christ and His disciples, through which He makes them share in His divine nature. This self-communication and participation, in its turn, must be made visibly present in the interhuman relationship, thus giving to the human reality a fulfillment and depth which goes far beyond the most daring human expectations.

Looking at the qualities of the love between the Father and the created world, St. John explains: "In this the love of God has been shown in our case, that God has sent His only-begotten son into the world that we may live through Him. In this is the love, not that we have loved God, but that He has first loved us, and sent His son a propitiation for our sins" (1 Jn 4:8–10). In these few sentences we find in a concise manner, but complete, everything we have mentioned as the elements of human love. There is the care and concern of God for humanity and the response to the human needs; there is God's all-pervading knowledge of humanity, but also His respect for the human personalities in that He lets them be in their own human way the visible translation of His invisible reality. This is true to such an extent that the love of God cannot exist in a human being if he does not have a real love for his fellow man: "For how can he who does not love his brother whom he sees, love God whom he does not see?" (1 Jn 4:20). The expression of love itself must be personal, respectful and fulfilling, for Christ said that we must love our neighbor as ourselves. If we assume that the individual human being has as his first concern his own existence, welfare and development, then this same concern is to be shown to the fellowman. The neighbor's development as a person must be close to the heart of everyone.

This expression of love concerns the human reality and dignity. It is not based upon any social equality as St. Paul says: "For all are children of God through faith in Christ Jesus. . . . (Before Christ) there is neither Jew nor Greek: there is neither slave nor free man; there is neither male nor female" (Gal. 3:26–28). The same interhuman relationship about which we have spoken earlier is transformed by faith into the visible manifestation of God's love for humanity.

One of the specific aspects of God's love is His acceptance and understanding of human limitation and weakness. He demonstrated this abundantly in His readiness to forgive. He Himself assumed human nature as "propitiation for our sins." While we were sinners and children of wrath, He claimed us as His beloved children. He forgave us and demands from men that they, too, will forgive those who trespass against them in an unlimited display of forgiving up to "seventy times seven," thus making the human limit as unlimited as His heavenly Father's (Mt. 18:35). Only in this fullness of self-giving, respect, responsibility and acceptance of our fellowman can we become the full expression of humanity for which God has laid the potential in every human being, namely, the sharing in the life of God Himself, for "he who abides in love abides in God and God in him" (1 Jn 4:16).

3. Human Love Demands Bodily Expression

At the beginning of this chapter we said that love is the "attitude of the human being by which he gives the proper value-response to another person." I think this expression is correct, but it should not be misunderstood. An attitude is a condition of the human mind, but the human person is much more than only a human mind. He has a "corporeal-spiritual" existence. This means he consists of body and spirit, not as two independent realities which eventually could exist on their own, but—in a way which no human mind has ever fully fathomed—the body is alive and is human only because it is animated by the spirit; while by the same token, the spirit exists and is present in this world only because it is united with the body. Spirit and body are aspects of the same human reality, and in their unity form the human person. Human love is the expression of the person, and only if it finds its concrete realization in some sort of perceptible form can it become meaningful as an interhuman communication. In a certain sense we can say that the innermost human feelings of appreciation and respect must be "materialized" before they can be considered as expressions of human love.

But the human expression is itself a mysterious happening. When we encounter a living human being, we will never say that we encountered a body; rather, we encountered a human person, but at the same time we do not know the depth of this human person. The same body which reveals to us the presence of our fellow man also hides his presence. The same happens in human actions. They reveal the inner feelings and attitudes of the other and, at the same time, they hide their most profound depth.

The depth of the inner human reality and its external expression do not necessarily coincide, for they are not the same. Just as body and spirit cannot exist independently but do not coincide, so also the human action does not exist independently from the human spirit, but it does not coincide with it. In a certain way we can call human action a materialization of a spiritual reality. But in so far as this materialization also hides the inner reality, it can be misused by the human person, and instead of being self-communication it can become a disguised form of selfishness; the other person is used as an "object" for one's own pleasure instead of being an expression of concern and care for the other. Then even the expression of love can become a downgrading of the other's human dignity.

Since the perceptible communication between persons lies in something external, it is also in something external that one searches for ways to please others and for ways to protect oneself. When people are truly honest, there exists a proper balance between their internal attitude and their external expressions; they can respect and trust each other's expression. Then they can properly grow and mature. But in ordinary human intercommunication one should keep in mind that dishonesty in one person provokes dishonesty in the other as a protective device for his own security and well-being.

Love is the most difficult art of human existence because of the complexity of the human being. Since love in its total expression is at the same time and in the same action both a total self-giving *and* a personal fulfillment, it is very difficult to discern whether a certain action is motivated by true love or by disguised selfishness. It might help to ask oneself whether the real reason for the action is the fulfillment of one's own need or a response to the need of the other.

4. The Meaning of Conjugal Love

If we can accept that marriage is at the same time both a "human reality" and a "sacrament of sanctification and redemption," then conjugal love also, which is the core of this reality, must have all the elements of human as well as of Christian (and sanctifying) love. There is no doubt that marriage is an interpersonal relationship, and as such it is subject to all the advantages and disadvantages of any other human relationship. It does have some extra advantages, however, because of the deeper knowledge which the partners obtain of each other. This gives them a better insight into their mutual needs and it increases the possibility of more appropriate responses to these needs. A fuller knowledge can increase the mutual respect, and thus give greater confidence for mutual reliance and support.

But all these advantages can turn into as many disadvantages, especially since the original mutual "external" attraction may have blinded the partners to each other's possible limitations, and then the ensuing disappointment might further blind them to the true human values which are really there but hidden. But if anywhere in human existence the axiom holds that "we must love our neighbor as ourselves," then, let us remember, that the marriage partner is in all circumstances the "nearest neighbor." In marriage this axiom receives a special depth and meaning, because not only is the partner the "nearest neighbor," but also the couple together form one source and principle of cooperation and development. They are "two in one flesh." With this in mind, Paul could say: "Husbands ought to love their wives as their own bodies," and "he who loves his own wife, loves himself" (Eph. 5:29). To the extent that the common task has become an inseparable aspect of their human fulfillment, the mutual love becomes an indispensable element in their own growth toward maturity.

Just as the human expression of love is so much more intimate in marriage so also must the Christian, the sanctifying aspect of love be more profound. It is here again that we go back to St. Paul:

Husbands should love their wives just as Christ loved the Church and sacrificed Himself for her, to make her holy. He made her clean by washing

her in water with a form of words, so that when
He took her to Himself she would be glorious
with no speck or wrinkle or anything like that,
but holy and faultless (Eph. 5:25–28).

Since human closeness provides the opportunity
for greater mutual openness, an opportunity is
provided for a total response in self-giving (sacri-
ficing one's self) and consequently for the greatest
increase in personal and mutual maturation and
development, and hence for greater sanctification
and more perfect expression of the total self-giving
of Christ to His Church and the human response to
God. Briefly we might say that conjugal love, correctly understood, is Christian love in a very real
sense.

But Christian expression of love in marriage
has one basic difference from any other form of
Christian love, namely, that ultimately it is based
upon the differentiation of sexes. Both partners
express by their very approach to each other the
biblical word: "It is not good for man to be
alone." In the final analysis, the man loves the
woman because of her femininity, and the woman
loves the man because of his masculinity. This is
the basic value, the special gift of the Creator to
each of them. All the further reasons and circumstances which bring them together, which make
them adapt to one another, which holds them together and brings them to a greater "one-ness" at
every moment of their lives, all are based upon

this original and basic need which the male and female ways of being-man have for each other.[5]

Upon this basis they feel their mutual needs. Upon this foundation they discover their mutual response-ability and they understand their mutual responsibility. Upon this same ground they grow in mutual respect and knowledge. Their whole life together in its human and Christian dimensions is built upon the differentiation of sexes. It would seem therefore that this specific aspect of the marital interrelationship deserves special attention.

[5] We do not suggest that men and women would not be complete as persons without each other. We only want to indicate that the differentiation of sexes is the ultimate basis of the mutual attraction of the spouses. It is a gift of the Creator for the good of humanity and for the sanctification of the spouses themselves. All other considerations go beyond the scope of this book.

Chapter Three

CONJUGAL LOVE AND THE DIFFERENTIATION OF THE SEXES

1. The Source of Strength in Today's Marriage

Conjugal love, we said, is a specific form of human and Christian love, and the specialty of this love consists in this that conjugal love, in the final analysis, is based upon the differentiation of sexes. When we look at today's divorce rate we may wonder what is going on in the present world. Not only is the absolute number of divorces higher today than some decades ago, but also the percentage of divorces in relation to the marriages contracted is on the increase.

We may try to assign the blame for this to whatever authority or whatever structure we want. One may blame the civil authorities because they make it easier today to get a divorce. Others may blame the low standards of morality in the present world and specifically the stress which is placed on sex and sexuality in today's advertising, films and publications. We may also blame the mentality among so many Catholics and perhaps also among priests who, in the presentation of the various aspects of human sexuality, take a more liberal stand than they used to take.

It would seem to me that until we start focusing our attention on the relationship between husband and wife in marriage, we are off target. The real strength and the real stability of marriage is to be found in the relationship between husband and wife. As a psychologist points out,

> There are two expectations with which most people go into marriage today:
> (a) the hope for regular sex satisfaction;
> (b) the hope for the enjoyments of a secure and intimate companionship and love.
> Often they don't get either.
> These two goals are not only intimately related to each other but also to the general personality patterns and life expectations of the married partners.[1]

The couples themselves enter into marriage with certain expectations and these expectations are of crucial importance. Often their "Yes, I will" to the question of the priest or minister has a totally different meaning in their minds and is much less based upon a total irrevocability than it used to be in the past. If we want to come to grips with this whole situation, it would seem to me, we must clearly keep at least two points in mind.

[1] Albert Ellis and Robert A. Harper, *Creative Marriage*, Lyle Stuart, New York, 1961, p. 17.

The first point is that we are living in a world of changing social structures, with all the advantages and disadvantages which this involves. And these global changes affect the marriage structure. Despite the intimate relationship between man and woman in marriage itself, marriage can never be considered outside the general social structure. As Ellis and Harper say in their book, CREATIVE MARRIAGE,

> The whole of modern social life of which marriage is an integral part, is today in such a state of rapid change and complex confusion that many personal goals and desires tend to be swept away in the general cultural storm.

> Since every couple and every marriage are part of the large society in which we live, and since this society is notoriously in a state of severe turmoil, it would be strange indeed to find that most people today were living in a state of effortless marital bliss.[2]

We cannot expect today that marriage will be easy. In today's changing world we see mainly the individual family pattern. This is a part of the social structure. It throws the couple back upon themselves and takes away much of the social environment and security which there used to be in the patriarchal and/or matriarchal society or in an extended family. This isolation and independence puts all the pressures and tensions upon the

[2] *op.cit.* p. 20.

couple themselves and the marriage has to be sustained from intra-marital resources. This makes it harder. But, on the other hand, let us not forget that it offers also opportunities for greater personal development. It would seem that it offers the opportunity to become better persons and, therefore, to create better marriages, or at least more personal marriages.

The second point is the fact that love is primarily based upon the respect which one has for the other. There must be a deep personal respect, based on knowledge of the proper personal values of each of the partners, on the understanding of their needs, and on the will and ability to give a proper response to these values and these needs. It seems clear that this mutual response presupposes a basic openness to each other which is supported by a basic interest in each other's well-being and development.

Strange as it may seem, such basic mutual interest is too often lacking in many of today's marriages, because of the expectations, beliefs and attitudes which people bring to their marriage. These expectations, beliefs and attitudes are more often based upon one's personal and individual interests than on the interests of the other partner. Usually the young man and the young woman do love one another, but what comes first for them is that one wants to make the other happy because it makes himself (or herself) happy. He feels so good when he can do something for her. She, in turn, feels good if he does this for her. She allows him to do it and perhaps she can do something for him in return. This makes them happy, but their happiness is centered upon their "feeling good" each one for himself or for herself and, unless they can switch later from this "feeling good" each one for himself or for herself to making the other happy, no proper marital response can develop.

2. Two Complementary Ways of Being Human

We called conjugal love a special expression of Christian and human love, and said that the deepest reason for this love was the differentiation of sexes. On purpose we did not say "sexual differences," because this would draw our attention too much to the difference of physical structure. If we emphasize a specific aspect, if we limit sex to the structure of the body and the physical organism, then we are, in a certain way, distorting the human being, because sex concerns the whole person. Human beings are male or female in their whole body and in their whole personality. In marriage there is an exchange of values between two persons. Man and woman are each a true expression of human nature but in a different way. This expression is such that they have the same dignity, the same human value, and in addition are mutually complementary.

In marriage, when male and female come together, they approach each other as persons, but precisely as a person who is man and a person who is woman. In marriage it is an exchange of values, the man gives himself exactly as he is, as a man, and the woman as a woman. This exchange, the self-giving of the one to the other for the sake of the other, is not to make this woman more masculine or to make this man more feminine; the purpose of the mutual exchange is that he might make her a better woman and that she might make him a better man. Only when man and woman respond to each other's needs with respect for each other's personalities, so that they make each other grow *as man* and *as woman,* can we speak of conjugal love. Any other approach is an expression of selfishness and will ultimately be destructive of a true marital relationship.

To understand better the meaning of conjugal love it seems necessary to point briefly to the differences of expression in their "being human," in their being man and being woman. The personality expresses itself always according to the proper structure of the human being. This means according to his or her biological and psychological aspects or any other aspect which contributes to making him or her fully human. Each of these aspects has its value, and not a single aspect may be overlooked. As soon as we overemphasize the biological part or the psychological part, we will distort marriage because we distort the human being. In marriage, therefore, the physical aspects do have a great value, for it is through the physical appearance that they appeal to each other in the first place. They catch sight of the other person by way of his or her physical appearance and physical abilities. The body itself, the stature and the build, the difference of texture, the softness or firmness, the prettiness or handsomeness has an appeal to the other sex.

The body itself is, in a certain way, the expression of what the personality is. The appearance certainly is not to be identified with the personality, but the appearance does reveal something of it. It is easy to say, for instance, that whether boys grow their hair long or not, does not mean a thing. It does not mean there is anything wrong in it, I fully agree; but it does indicate something. Either they want to be different from others or they want to conform. This indicates something about their personality. So also, in a meeting between man and woman, the boy sees something in the girl, how she dresses and what she tries to convey through her manner of dressing. That she tries to convey to him her femininity is a very normal thing, but it is possible that the stress which she places on this is geared so much to an overemphasizing of the external that it might reveal a superficial personality, or a personality only concerned with herself.

On the other hand, a person who completely disregards his own dress and appearance, may well convey to the other that he or she is a person who doesn't care about anything whatsoever. External appearance is an important fact; it should not be overemphasized, of course, but it adds its weight to the balance and should be taken into consideration. If this figures into the initial approach between boy and girl, it counts also for husband and wife, because they should always remain a couple who are in love. If they want to grow in love from day to day, to know each other more intimately, they have to express this, and to convey this externally to the other.

Perhaps much more important than the physical expression is the psychological reality of the human being. Hardly anything could be more difficult than to try to describe with a measure of completeness the psychological differences between man and woman. I am not going to try to do this; too little is know with exactitude, and a description can never be complete. We can only give general characteristics and an outline of the psychology of man and woman. No individual details can be given here because every human being is different. The general difference between man and woman is manifest in the main human faculties of intellect, will and emotional life. In trying to describe this general tendency here, I'm not implying that one is superior to the other; they are just different and complementary. Let us thank God that no human creature exists which is purely male, and let us be equally grateful that there is no human creature which is purely female. In every person there is a certain combination of both elements, but a general predominant tendency can be traced in each sex.

The first aspect of the general difference concerns the *intellect*. In the man the general tendency of the intellect is directed toward a more objective judgment. He has a greater aptitude for finding means which help to accomplish a purpose, and greater ability to see through the individual particulars to the general outcome of a problem. His major orientation is to things outside himself. In the woman the intellect is differently oriented. She works more easily with a sort of intuitive knowledge. She has a greater feeling for the interior values of persons and things than for the objective structure. Her knowledge is more a connaturality with the object or person. It is more guided by feelings than by abstraction.

The second general area relates to the *will*. In the man we see more the tendency to conquer obstacles and to overcome resistance. He has the drive to possess and the urge to push through. He has his pride in accomplishing the undertakings which he has started. This makes him often less pliable to the needs of others, but it can also make him more vulnerable. The failure to accomplish his goals may well shake his self-esteem and injure his pride. This tendency to possess and to dominate can make him egotistic and thoughtless of others.

In the woman, the general tendency is different. Her strength lies more in a greater ability to submit to others and to serve others. It is not a slave-like subservience, but rather a service which is contributive and supporting, aiding the other to be himself or herself. It is the tendency of the mother to give life and to sustain life where it is in need or where it grows. Often she has an exceptional ability to endure suffering, but at the same time she asks for support. If the husband is too submissive to her, she may feel insecure and even stage an opposition to him to provoke him to take over the responsibility. The woman, too, can be egotistic and selfish, but it expresses itself differently than in the man. She gives herself totally, but she will demand the same of her husband—even to such an extent that she sometimes resents his extra-domestic activities, which she interprets as an infringement on his love for her.

As the third general area, we may look to human *affectivity*. With this I mean being influenced by emotions. The man is more critical. He is more alert to the usefulness of things and persons. His emotions are, as far as this is possible, at the service of his intellect and of his drive to accomplish things. He would rather use his affectivity to reach a goal than abandon himself to his emotions. His dedication to his wife and family is often expressed in his dedication to his job. The pride of success in his job intertwines with his pride in his family. The disadvantage of this is that he can become so involved in his professional duties that his family is reduced to being merely an accessory in his life.

The woman, on the other hand, will more easily abandon herself to her emotions. Consequently, she will have a greater aptitude for sacrificial love and self-giving. She feels a connaturality with the object which needs her dedication. Love penetrates her whole being. It is the primary need of her life. Everything that really touches her is experienced with heart and intellect, and she is totally occupied with it. This can express itself, for instance, very noticeably when there is a slight argument in the morning. The man promptly forgets the whole incident and is quite surprised to see after his day's work that it still occupies his wife's mind.

Not only does the woman have a natural tendency toward motherhood, but she also tends to commit herself totally to the new life. Her qualities of tenderness and detailed concern find their fulfillment in this task. But the care of her children may also alienate her from her husband, who may become in such a circumstance "the father of *her* children." In her affectivity the woman has her greatest vulnerability. Her totality of self-giving demands a response, and when this response does not measure up to her expectations, her life may be frustrated, and jealousy, suspicion, and similar feelings might soon embitter her.

It is obvious that these qualities hardly ever occur in their concrete and pure form. They are always subject to "more or less," but the general tendency in man and woman is usually noticeable. In the married life of the partners these qualities

interact and complement each other, provided
each partner has an openness for the needs of the
other. In conjugal love the man does not impose
his masculinity upon the woman, nor does she
impose upon her husband her femininity, but the
mutual exchange and the mutual concern balance
the tendencies toward extremes on either side.
Even when they are not actually together, the
spouses are present to each other, but this presence is different in each one. The wife is usually
surrounded with all sorts of things which remind
her of her husband, and a large segment of her
domestic duties are performed to make life pleas-
ant for him and to make the home a good place to
be in. The man is in a different situation. His work
occupies him, and though it is a highly important
aspect in his expression of concern for his family,
thoughts about his wife are usually pushed far
back from his immediate concern. It often demands an extra effort on his part to show her that
she was in his thoughts during the day. It can be
important for the marriage that he makes this effort.

3. Total Self-giving to Each Other

However important the man-woman relationship may be even in ordinary daily life, the most
intimate involvement of man and woman lies, no
doubt, in the marital relationship, called sexual
intimacy or sexual intercourse. This is not something marginal but a central point; we should keep

in mind, however, that it is not the only point. There is no relationship in marriage which more deeply involves the total human being and the total personality. It is not just a biological function. Husband and wife are totally as a man and totally as a woman involved in this specific act. It is the moment in which man and woman, who love each other dearly, give expression to their total self-giving to each other. The conjugal intimacy in its most intimate form is the expression of a total trust of one in the other. As Father Janssens points out, "Sexual intercourse is primarily a matter of trust. One completely abandons oneself to the other in actually giving oneself bodily."[3] Then he refers to the text of St. Paul:

Let the husband render to the wife her due, and likewise the wife to the husband. The wife has not authority over her body, but the husband; the husband likewise has not authority over his body, but the wife (1 Cor. 7:3–4).

It is a total giving of one to the other in which indeed two lives blend into one. It is this expression of love which is so extremely important. In a recent book Father Janssens states:

In the past the act of conjugal intimacy was primarily considered as a natural act in the service of procreation. The present day personalistic way

[3] L. Janssens, *Conjugal Morality*. Unpublished notes of 1964, p. 29.

of thinking, completely in accordance with the doctrine of Vatican Council II, stresses that conjugal intimacy because of its own internal meaning is an expression of conjugal love. It can, therefore, never be taken out of this context of conjugal love, but must be placed in the service of this specific human relationship.[4]

This point is very important. If we overstress the importance of sexual intercourse in marriage, then we make marriage a "place where we can have sexual intercourse"; this is degrading for the human person and for marriage. I am not at all belittling here the importance of sexual intercourse. I fully appreciate the great importance which it has if husband and wife can reach together the highest satisfaction of a simultaneous sexual orgasm. But however important this aspect may be, simultaneous orgasm does not guarantee that there is a real marital expression. A couple can also artificially learn to reach such an orgasm without there being a personal and mutual self-giving. Similarly, the absence of a simultaneous orgasm does not indicate that there is not a good and true mutual self-giving. The importance of simultaneous orgasm is great, but it is not the only thing that counts.

It is quite possible, we may say in this context, that in marriage there are acts which are not or

[4] L. Janssens, *Echtelijke Liefde en Verantwoord Ouderschap*, p. 143.

hardly above plain adulterous intercourse. It can happen that one partner simply imposes on the other his or her demand in an imperious way, and this would be a plain seeking of sexual self-satisfaction. Whenever self-satisfaction is the prime motive, we do not have the blending together of the two lives. It is the use of the other as an object for one's own self-satisfaction. This is degrading and downgrading for the other, especially in this relationship. We may take into account the words of Ignace Lepp:

> Of all the instincts the sexual is without doubt the one in which the psychological and biological are most interwoven. However, especially in the case of sex, it is necessary to take issue with the application to the human being of theories about the instincts of a purely biological nature. It would not even be true to say that sexuality constitutes a side of love that is physical.[5]

The couple must make this interrelationship between man and woman into something which is a *personal* relationship.

Since the differences between man and woman are so great, it can also easily happen that in the sexual relationship of a married couple each one is primarily concerned with his or her own interests and desires. It may seem to the woman that the

[5] Ignace Lepp, *The Psychology of Loving*, Helicon, 1964, p. 22.

man is selfish. It is often hard for her to understand how he can come so easily to sexual satisfaction. She is often surprised how little it means to
him to have further intimacies after he has
reached his orgasm. He has reached what he was
looking for and he comes to an almost complete
equilibrium. This is often felt by the woman as
something which is selfish. It might seem to her
that he is just looking out for himself, because he
leaves her alone while she is still in a completely
different stage. She doesn't feel that he cares for
her.

Yet, this is how the male constitution is, it is
easily aroused and quickly satisfied. When the
urge is not there, there is nothing further from his
mind than inter-sexual relations. The woman is
totally different; for her the sexual relation is not
something that can come up suddenly, it requires
a long preparation. For the woman it is, much
more than for the man, the total giving of the
whole personality. It might be that, after an argument, intercourse is simply disgusting to her even
if she would come to full sexual satisfaction; because it is the giving of herself to a person, who at
this moment, is not a person who is completely in
love with her. This is true unless they want to use
this approach to make up to each other and make
it the renewed expression of love. For the wife,
sexual desire is not something that comes up suddenly, but it demands a preparation that goes all
through the day. It is a constant awareness where-

in she, in her own personality as a woman, gives herself a long time before and a long time after. As Dr. Lips says in one of his books:

> The erotic love is a demand of the whole wo-man. Instead of sexual approach she asks for tenderness, continuous attention for her whole being, every day, every week, every month again. With this she could already be happy. Only when her erotic desires are satisfied in tenderness can she experience satisfaction in sexual intimacy. The woman cannot live in marriage without this erotic love. Her desires and needs would remain unfulfilled.[6]

This is something which a man might easily forget, because his whole life is oriented to his job. There is a danger that sensitivity to his wife's needs becomes something marginal in marriage, and nothing could be more disastrous than this. The psychological union is the most important for the woman. The sexual union is incorporated into this and is a completion of it. Without this psychological and personal union the sexual intimacy is less important for her. Let us try to understand how extremely important this difference between man and woman is in their mutual relationship in marriage itself.

We may begin by stating what the Church teaches in this matter. We can understand why the

[6] Dr. A. C. M. Lips, *Mens Zijn in het Huwelijk,* Romen & Zonen, Roermond-Maaseik, 1966, p. 17.

Church stresses the totality of marriage, which is a total giving of life in which the one complements the other, in which the man becomes a better man by making her a better woman by understanding her and supporting her in her role as a woman, and vice versa. The act of sexual intimacy is the expression of the totality. As soon as we take it out of this totality, we are disrupting and distorting marriage itself. Outside of marriage, sexual intimacy loses its deeply human meaning. It is about these specific acts that the Vatican Council II says:

> The actions within marriage by which the couple are united intimately and chastely are noble and worthy ones. Expressed in a manner which is truly human, these actions promote that mutual self-giving by which spouses enrich each other with joyful and ready will (*The Church in the Modern World,* No. 49).

The Council sees these acts as an enrichment for each other in which they become better human beings. Then the Council goes on:

> The acts themselves which are proper to conjugal love and which are exercised in accord with genuine human dignity must be honored with great reverence (*Ibid.,* No. 51).

We can now see the danger of defining marriage as a contract between a man and a woman in which each one gives the other the right to such acts which by their nature are directed to the procreation of children. If we are not very careful, we could degrade this most sacred intimacy in marriage and make this most intimate giving of one person to the other the business of a contract, a sort of right to demand. But as soon as the right is demanded in marriage against the will of the other, who may have good reason for not responding at this moment, this demand is an infringement upon the growth in love. For this reason mutual understanding is so important.

It may happen that the woman does not feel inclined to sexual intercourse at this moment, but she knows her husband. She knows how he feels and what his needs are; and, because of love for him she might, and often she can, be completely willing and even desiring to have conjugal intimacy because she knows that she will thus be a support to his personal development. On the other hand, the man, although he may desire intercourse at a certain moment, may know that for a good reason it would not be fair to his partner, and therefore he abstains from it because of love for her. Because of respect for her personality as a woman, and because of his respect for the totality of marriage, he can have and must have enough strength to bear this sacrifice himself. Then the abstention can become an expression of love and respect and contribute to the mutual growth of both.

This differentiation of sexes plays an important role in the reality of the sacrament of marriage. It is the basic factor which makes the total life of the partners fuse into one great unity. When they express in this relationship their deep respect and love for one another and display for the good of each other this deep sense of sacrifice, then this mutual exchange becomes the living expression of Christ's total self-giving to the Church—the People of God—and the Church's response to Christ. Just as the love of Christ to the Church is sanctifying and redeeming, so also is the love between the spouses. Just as the love of Christ is constantly fruitful by communicating His divine life to humanity, so also is the love between the spouses by its nature fruitful by communicating new life to each other and to others.

Chapter Four

"CONJUGAL LOVE WHICH BY
ITS NATURE IS FRUITFUL"

With infinite wisdom the Creator expressed the purpose of creation in created existence itself. He also gave to humanity the ability and the responsibility to search for this purpose, to discover it and to live by it according to the divine plan. He granted to man more than just existence he destined him for more than blindly following the forces of material creation; he gave man the power "to participate in divine providence in the sense that man is able to take care of himself and of others."[1]

It is in the divine plan that man voluntarily and by free acts sets the course of his life toward God.[2] In this task of search and discovery God Himself aids man with His divine revelation. First, He has given to man his intellect, which, as an imprint of the divine light in us, makes it possible for man to carry out this search and to discover the purpose

[1] Thomas Aquinas, *S. T.*, p. I–II, q. 91, a. 2.
[2] *Declaration on Religious Freedom*, No. 3.

of his own existence. A specific and very important aspect of this search of man for the purpose
of his existence is the search for the meaning and
the purpose of marriage, so that in this discovery
man might be able to recognize the responsibility
which this state of life imposes upon him.

Marriage is part of human life and part of the
expression of human dignity. But human life and
human dignity have not been revealed to mankind
in one all-embracing act of revelation nor have
they been understood in one act of human insight,
but it is in a progressive self-unfolding throughout
the various stages of human history that man has
come to an ever deeper understanding and appreciation of what he is and of what his responsibilities are. But within this evolutionary process,
mankind as a whole never lost sight of man's basic
directedness to God. Similarly, in the various approaches to, and developmental stages of the understanding of the meaning and purpose of marriage man never lost sight of its basic orientation.
On the contrary, aided by divine revelation, man
even went beyond the understanding which
seemed to be implied in the more or less immediately apparent satisfaction of evident human
needs in conjugal living.

As we have mentioned earlier, throughout the
various stages of development in the successive
eras of human history, marriage has remained an
earthly reality. The different approaches to, and
the insights into its purpose and meaning, the

changes which came about did not touch the essence of marriage itself, but they were a progressive development achieved by the human mind which "gradually and more precisely lays bare the laws of society."[3] The People of God take part in this discovery. Their contribution to it should perhaps be more decisive than anybody else's, because they "believe that they are led by the Lord's Spirit who fills the earth, and motivated by this faith they labor to decipher the authentic signs of God's presence and purpose in the happenings, needs and desires which they share along with other people of their age."[4]

Earlier we tried to explain how marriage is a gift of God to man with the purpose of procreating the human race and guiding its cultural development. We endeavored to show how this original gift came to be understood as the visible expression of God's salvific love for mankind in the redemptive action of Christ. We discussed how this human love evolved into a deep Christian love while it remained based upon the differentiation of sexes according to the plan of the Creator. It would, then, be an unfaithfulness to the Creator Himself if we disregarded the various stages of development. Hidden underneath the obscuring multitude of human expressions, covered with the veil of human successes and failures the golden

[3] *Pastoral Constitution on the Church in the Modern World,* No. 4.
[4] *Ibid.,* No. II.

thread of God's plan can be discovered in the developmental process that has gone on till the present day. Basing ourselves upon its discovery, we can continue the task of seeking to come to an ever deeper understanding of God's plan with humanity. With this in mind, we continue to search for the meaning of marriage as conjugal love which by its nature is fruitful. Our search leads us to consider man's dignity in the perspective of its historical development.

"A sense of the dignity of the human person has been impressing itself more and more deeply on the consciousness of contemporary man,"[5] and it is this same sense of the dignity of the human person which forms the background against which today's man can understand the meaning and the purpose of marriage. If man is indeed the human person who is by his nature the inseparable unity of spirit and body, then the purpose and meaning of marriage must lie in the expression of this totality. It would be an insult to the human person to make his marriage exclusively subject to the biological laws of irrational nature. However hidden, this human dignity has always been the warp upon which the patterns of marriage were woven.

1. Marriage and Personal Dignity in the Old Testament

At the beginning of creation God saw that "it was not good for man to be alone" and He made

[5] *Declaration on Religious Freedom*, No. I.

him a helper like himself. The intention was apparently the well-being and development of the human person. Man and woman were destined to cling to each other. Together they were blessed, together they received the task to cultivate the earth and to subdue it, to have dominion over all creatures, to become one flesh—one principle and source of operation—to multiply and to fill the earth. The task was all-embracing. It included, we may say, to give the finishing touches to creation, to make the earth a place worthy for man to live in and to procreate men who would live in this place and continue the same task. All these various aspects blend together into one great task.

The fulfillment of it is human dignity, which includes in its essence the continuation of human existence. But where the Old Testament describes the task which the Creator gave to men, it does not mention a variety of purposes which can be considered independently. The creation-narratives present cultural development and procreation as one unit. The revelation in the prophetic books, in which marriage is spoken of as the expression of God's love for his people, also combines love and procreation, and in various places where offspring is praised as the greatest blessing of Yahweh, it still is seen within the bond of conjugal unity and love. When Onan was punished because of his wilful rejection of procreation, it was not because of interrupting the sexual intimacy, but because of his refusal to fulfill the law which was the expres-

sion of the convenant between Yahweh and his
people.

With regard to the moral evaluation of sexuality, in the Old Testament we see derision for the
prostitute who decorates herself and walks the
streets to draw the attention of men whom she can
seduce; we read of contempt for the man who
follows her as one who is led as "an ox to the
slaughter." On the other hand, we are struck by
the respect and joy shown toward romance in the
Canticle of Canticles, where the young man and
the maiden long for each other and search for
each other in a love which is unselfish and pure.
The man-woman relationship is presented to us as
beautiful and good where it is unselfish and en-
hances the dignity of man; but by the same token
it is rejected and despised when its only purpose is
selfish and pleasure seeking.

2. Marriage and Personal Dignity in the New Testament

The Gospels and the other New Testament
writings endorse what the Old Testament transmitted to them about marriage, its meaning and
earthly reality. Christ stresses its indissolubility
and St. Paul points out how this hearth of human
love is in Christian dimensions the expression of
Christ's redemptive love for the Church. So great
is the emphasis on love in marriage in the New
Testament that it could even mislead us and make
us think that the mutual love of the spouses is the

primary reason why marriage exists. But when the New Testament speaks about marriage, it takes the whole concept as it was handed over by the Old Testament. Procreation was taken for granted as an indispensable part of marriage; for instance, when the Gospel speaks of the joy over a child born into the world (Jn 16:21), or when St. Paul says that the married woman shall be saved by giving birth to children (1 Tim. 2:15, 5:14). But all this was understood within the context of the normal marital perspective known to the culture of that time, this means, within the context of the same understanding of human dignity.

But St. Paul gives us also a little insight into what is, in his understanding of the Christian doctrine, the importance of conjugal intimacy in marriage. His followers in Corinth had asked him: "Is it good for a man not to touch a woman?" Whether they asked this in view of the importance of virginity, or whether it was a question about the advisability of not having relations in marriage, is not known. But St. Paul's answer is clear in relation to either question.

It is good for man not to touch woman. Yet, for fear of fornication, let each man have his own wife, and let each woman have her own husband. Let the husband render to the wife her due, and likewise the wife to the husband. The wife has not authority over her body, but the husband; the husband likewise has not authority over his

82   GOD'S LOVE IN HUMAN LANGUAGE

cept perhaps by consent, for a time, that you
may give yourselves to prayer; and return together again lest Satan tempt you because you
lack self-control. But this I say by way of con-
cession, not by way of commandment. For I
would that all were as I myself; but each one has
his own gift from God, one in this way and
another in that (I Cor. 7:1–7).

When we place St. Paul's words in their historical context, we can see his profound understanding of man. The City of Corinth had both a very
loose morality among a large section of the popu-
lation and a severe ascetism under the influence of
Stoic philosophy in another group, who considered any indulgence in material satisfaction as an
evil and as unworthy of man's dignity. Paul de-
fends the goodness of conjugal intimacy as a req-
uisite for their mutual fidelity and as in no way
contrary to the dignity of man. But on the other
hand, he points out that conjugal intimacy at any
time is not the sole purpose of marriage; it is good
also to abstain from it, especially to direct the
mind to prayer.

We should take into account how the philosophy of that time saw man as a duality of body and
spirit. It did not understand the unity of the
human person as we do today. To what extent
Paul directed himself against this philosophy is
hard to say, but he certainly wanted to convey to
his readers the understanding that also in their

marital relationship their life could and should be directed to God. Temporary abstinence was not by the choice of the individual partner but only by mutual agreement. And when the human urge or need would be too strong to cope with, so that Satan could tempt their fidelity, they ought to come together again to express their love and unity. No mention is made of the relationship between conjugal intimacy and procreation. This matter did not come up. We must assume that this was simply regarded as an integral part of marriage, especially since offspring was so often praised as a special blessing of God.

Perhaps we are reading in Paul's letter more than he ever had in his mind, but it seems to me that Paul was concerned with the dignity of the human being and his relationship to God in marriage. He gave the same explicit indication in a letter to his collaborator Timothy. Paul warns him against false tendencies which will creep up among Christians. Some will say: "Marriage is forbidden," but Paul reminds him that "every thing God has created is good" (1 Tim. 4:3). Again, he takes marriage as a totality and as a special gift of God to men, in which unity and procreation are inseparably united.

3. Theological Developments About Marriage and Man's Personal Dignity

While procreation was unqualifiedly accepted as an integral part of marriage in the Old Testament and during the apostolic era, it seems to have become a problem of rather wide dimensions by the time of St. Augustine. The tendencies against which St. Paul wrote in his letters to the Christians in Corinth and to Timothy had increased in strength by the time of Augustine. Augustine himself was educated in Greek and Roman philosophy and his thinking was strongly influenced by it. In the Neo-platonic and especially in the Stoic philosophy, the dignity of man was identified with the rule of the spirit over the body. Every loss of this command of the spirit over the body was an insult to man and unworthy of his human dignity, and therefore also sexual intercourse with its resulting orgasm was below the dignity of man.

In this same period the heresy of the Manichaeans proclaimed that in man only the spirit was good and that the body was totally evil. It was a punishment for the human spirit to be in the body and consequently procreation was an evil because it perpetuated this diabolical situation. Intercourse itself was already bad enough, but intercourse resulting in procreation was the work of the devil.

Against this background St. Augustine took his position. Accepting the superiority of the spirit over the body, especially in the Christian perspective wherein we know and love God with our spirit, he rejected the position of the Manichaeans and proclaimed that marriage and procreation were good and holy. Faithful to his philosophy of the superiority of the spirit over the body—viewed in the perspective of the dualism of body and spirit —he saw in the unity of marriage primarily a spiritual unity for the growth and perfection of the spouses (the *bonum fidei*). Because of their baptism and union with Christ, this unity was a symbol of stability (*bonum sacramenti*) which could never be broken. Within this unbreakable unity procreation was to take place. But procreation itself was in the mind of St. Augustine—as it was in the mind of all his contemporaries—a biological process which had a value in itself apart from the union in love between the spouses. In fact, the procreation was seen by him as the basic reason which justified conjugal intimacy and, apart from procreation, conjugal intimacy always to a certain extent fell short of human dignity.

However severe Augustine's judgment may seem to be, if we see it in the total philosophical understanding of human nature at that specific time, then we see that his main concern was not the biological process, but the dignity of man. The biological function took a very important place in his understanding of marriage, but this was never seen in a context in which man was directed by the laws of biology; rather biology took its place in the concept of human dignity, especially with regard to the union of men and their relation to God.

St. Augustine's vision on marriage has influenced all Christian thinking up to our present day, but within the boundaries of his concepts many phases of development have taken place. Another important milestone is found in St. Thomas Aquinas, some 800 years later. Aquinas based his philosophy largely on Aristotle. In Aristotle's vision the world of living creatures was divided into a multitude of various kinds. All living beings had many aspects in common; other aspects were found only in some particular living beings. For Aristotle and later for Aquinas, the realm of life was an ascending scale from the common to the specialized. The more perfectly developed creatures had all that was in the lower kinds, but in addition they had something that was found only in them.

This view led Thomas to study first what is common to all—this is the generic aspect—and only thereafter that which is specific for the next step. But it was not at any time his intention to say that every creature had first to fulfill the demands of its generic existence and then only subsequently the demands of its specific way of being. Rather, what Aquinas wanted to say—and indeed did say —was that the generic dimension was to be lived in the specific way of the individual creature. For example, the human being has all the components of many animals, but he is specified by the fact that he has reason. Man is therefore a rational animal. This did not mean in Aquinas' mind that the first requirement in man is to fulfill all the animal requirements and that then only reason entered the field to give this animal life a special flavor; rather he said that man must live his life, which is in many respects so much like the life of an animal, in a specifically human way.

In relation to marriage also the whole meaning of the bodily structure was integrated in the totality of the "human existence." It had to be lived "in a human way." He described marriage as "an association of life between man and woman which is directed toward sexual community and everything connected therewith."[6] He distinguishes in marriage the task of nature, which he sees as the biological function, and the task of man, which refers to the way in which this task is to be fulfilled. But for Aquinas this distinction does not constitute a duality; rather it blends together into a unity and thus constitutes the dignity of the human person. It is the association of life between the two sexes, based upon this differentiation of sexes which includes mutual fulfillment and procreation as one inseparable unity.

The Augustinian influence was still there and Aquinas was not too sure that conjugal intimacy apart from the procreative aspects was entirely good, but he was much less strict than St. Augustine. However, the basic concern of both was the same, namely, the dignity of man as created by God and on his way to God.

These two giants of Christian thinking (Augus-

[6] *In IV Sent.*, d. 2, a. 4.

tine and Aquinas) laid the foundation for later development. In the fifteenth century some courageous theologians started to defend the thesis that conjugal intimacy even apart from the context of procreation was not sinful. Mutual assistance in marriage and the task to relieve human concupiscence were seen as a superadded purpose in the marital union. They were expressions protecting mutual fidelity and love and, as such, they were good.

We should not underestimate the enormous step which these theologians made. During that time, and even until the end of the nineteenth century, it was generally thought that human procreation came from a germ contained in the male seed, and that the female role was limited to providing the fertile nourishing ground in which this seed had to be planted and could grow. The loss of the male seed therefore was the loss of the human life. But still, in the marital context and for the sustainment of marital love and unity, sexual intimacy was seen as good and in conformity with the dignity of human existence as it was in this world.

It is understandable that in this light the biological structure of the conjugal act receives a particular importance. On the one hand, the need for conjugal intimacy was recognized even if no procreation was to follow; on the other hand, there was the frustration of the biological process which, in their eyes, was the frustration of human life, for they thought that such a life was germinally but completely present in the male sperm, which was purposely prevented from developing. In this light to purposely frustrate intercourse was regarded as a form of homicide. So we can understand how the biological aspects of conjugal intimacy had a special importance. The "natural orientation of the act" and the "openness to procreation" received a special biological meaning and a value which was entirely based upon the biological functioning of the human being. This approach, together with the accepted duality of body and soul in man, explains their attitude toward marital intercourse. However, within this scheme we see again that their main concern was not the biological structure for its own sake, but their concern was the full protection of the dignity of the human person in his totality.

Though the understanding of the mutually complementary role of man and woman in procreation became better understood at the turn of the century, the dualistic understanding of man had not yet been overcome. In the Encyclical *Casti Connubii* Pope Pius XI was still completely under the influence of the earlier approach to the understanding of marriage. He distinguishes sharply between the primary purpose, "marriage in a more restricted sense as an institute to procreate and educate children," and the secondary ends, "marriage in a wider sense as a community for life."

We see here the Augustinian approach which places the two goals of marriage side by side without real integration. The biological aspects and organic functioning received the major stress as it had in past centuries, no longer because the male sperm was regarded as self-sufficient, but now it was based upon a misinterpretation of Aquinas' concept of "natural law." This misinterpretation saw the purely biological pattern as the manifestation of the will of the Creator. Every infringement on it was then necessarily a serious transgression of the law of God. Consequently, we have in this encyclical the absolute prohibition against any artificial means of birth regulation, under threat of mortal sin.

That this aspect received so much stress was undoubtedly partly due to the fact that the social structure of marriage had by then solidly entered into the "individual family pattern," in which the extension of the family often caused problems. The main concern of *Casti Connubii* was then again the respect for human dignity, but from a viewpoint which is alien to our time. Even though in the language of biology, the core of its teaching was man's dignity and, as such, *Casti Connubii* was one step further along toward a fuller and better understanding. One positive and valuable aspect we must not overlook in the encyclical is that it was the first time that an official ecclesiastical document pointed out that mutual love of the spouses is an integral (though not essential) aspect of marriage.

Pope Pius XII took another step in this devel-

opment. He underlined over and again the principles laid down by his predecessor, but in his teaching we see one point emerging into the
foreground, namely, the essential importance of
love in marriage. Though he tried to escape the
dualistic conception of man, a perception of the
unity of the human person had not yet sufficiently
ripened to penetrate his whole teaching.

It was during Vatican Council II that this idea
finally found its way into Catholic theology. Here
we find an approach which takes the person as a
totality, not as a sort of composition of two elements, the soul and the body, but as an integrated
reality which is, at the same time, corporeal and
spiritual. This has enormous consequences for the
understanding of human dignity and of the human
relationship to God. Human dignity is not constituted by the spirit dominating the body, but the
total existential reality in its corporeal-spiritual
unity is the subject of human actions. The body is
not a mere tool in the hand of the spirit, nor does
it have its own independent purpose alongside the
purpose of the human spirit.

With respect to marriage this means that we
can no longer speak of a primary and secondary
end in marriage, the procreation of children on
the one hand, and the spiritual union of the couple
on the other. These two flow together into a one-
ness. The act of conjugal intimacy is an unbreakable one-ness which at the same time is both uniting
in love and procreative. Never before in history

have ecclesiastical documents spoken with so much openness and with so much frankness about the sexual relationship between the spouses. The Council says:

> The actions within marriage by which the couple are united intimately and chastely are noble and worthy ones. Expressed in a manner which is truly human, these actions promote that mutual self-giving by which spouses enrich each other with a joyful and ready will (*The Church in the Modern World,* No. 49).

But also in the view of Vatican Council II the love of the spouses, however important it may be, is not the only aspect of the total human being. By command of the Creator, their task is not only to cultivate and enrich the pre-given world, but in a very true sense they are co-creators with God and the dispensers of His love to humanity, and therefore:

> While not making the other purposes of matrimony of less account, the true practice of conjugal love and the whole meaning of family life which results from it, have this aim: that the couple be ready with stout hearts to cooperate with the love of the Creator and the Savior, who through them will enlarge and enrich his family day by day" (*Ibid.,* No. 50).

Thus the whole human being in his corporeal and spiritual existence blends into a unity of expression which cannot be broken. To show still more clearly that these two aspects do not stand apart as individual responsibilities, the Council says a little later:

> Marriage to be sure is not instituted solely for procreation; rather, its very nature as an unbreakable compact between persons, and the welfare of the children, both demand that the mutual love of the spouses be embodied in a rightly ordered manner, that it grow and ripen (*Ibid.*, No. 50).

Here the Council points emphatically to the meaning of the embodiment of conjugal love as an expression of the dignity of the human persons who are involved. But the love which must exist between the couple is integrally one with the existence and welfare of the children. In this totality the continuation and increase of love and the embodiment of love belong to the total realization of human dignity.

The Council realized that in the totality of this expression all the human elements are involved, that is, man, with his spirit and with his body. On purpose therefore the Council abstained from making any comparison between the different values, be they biological, psychological or sociological. It recognized that all belong to man and that none of them is accidental to man, all belong to the essence of man's life on earth. How these various values, or various aspects in human and marital existence should be preserved and how they interact in the different circumstances of life was left for further study and for final decision by the Pope.

After a long period of deliberation, the Pope finally has given his decision on this point in his encyclical *On Human Life*. The first reading of the encyclical may give the impression that the Pope presents only a part of the total view on marriage. He seems to focus on the importance of the biological structures, and he stresses that these may never be violated. If this first impression were correct the encyclical would be a very one-sided document which would be deeply confusing for the non-expert, and for the expert it would be hard to swallow.

An additional difficulty for the theologian is that the Pope bases his argumentation upon natural law. The concept of natural law which he uses does not seem to go beyond the concept of biological structures which man can discover with his intellect and which he is then bound to follow. The majority of today's theologians no longer admit this specific understanding of natural law. For them natural law is a dynamic reality in man which encompasses the human being as a whole and which goes far beyond biological structures. A more penetrating study of the encyclical we will reserve for a later discussion. But whatever our appreciation of the encyclical may be, we should never overlook the positive point which it presents, namely, that physiological integrity is part of the total integrity of the conjugal intimacy and that, therefore, it belongs to the dignity of the human person of which Vatican Council II speaks.

For the moment it is important to see why I have spent so much time in tracing the history regarding the development of the understanding of human dignity. I think it is important that we see man as a totality. This totality has always been there, but since man is by his nature corporeal-spiritual, there has been a tendency to focus on one side or the other. To find a balance is the task of human life on earth. The search has been going on since the origin of mankind, and it has not yet been completed.

Our time is participating most importantly in this search, and unless we thoroughly understand that man's dignity consists in this that his life on earth is directed to God precisely in its earthly reality—that human life is the manifestation of God's presence in this universe—unless we keep this in mind, we are likely to disregard certain aspects of the human reality. We then might end up with overemphasizing earthly attractions at the cost of the real dignity of man. Only if we fully understand that conjugal love is by its nature fruitful, will we be able to discuss what moral responsibilities this fruitful love places upon man in marriage.

Chapter Five

FRUITFUL LOVE AND
MORAL RESPONSIBILITY

In the foregoing reflections I have tried to convey two concepts which are most intimately interwoven, namely:

1. Conjugal love is the expression of the total human being in marriage and is therefore based upon the dignity of man.

2. This conjugal love by its nature is fruitful.

1. Fruitfulness

It is the word "fruitfulness" which concerns us here. It would be too simple to understand fruitfulness exclusively as "giving birth to children." This certainly is a form of fruitfulness, but generation is a biochemical process. However important the biochemical and biological aspects in human existence may be, they can never be identified with human existence. If we wish to speak of fruitfulness in relation to man, it will be necessary to speak about it in its total human context, which includes all human relationships and responsibilities. For the sake of clarity, I want to indicate three different aspects of human fruitfulness, not as if these aspects exist (or even can exist) separately in a human couple, but as aspects of the same fruitfulness. In other words, all three aspects should be present in the same human reality if we want to speak about fruitfulness in its complete and human form.

1. Marriage is a form of self-giving between husband and wife: "for this reason the man . . . will cling to his wife." In this mutual self-giving there is an enrichment and ennobling of the partners themselves. Each partner makes the other partner a better human being, and by doing so becomes a more perfect (mature) human being himself or herself. This development is growth; it is produced, and it can in a very real sense be seen as a form of fruitfulness which is specifically human.

2. The self-giving of husband and wife, especially in the act of conjugal intimacy, is total and unreserved. It is the giving of one's life and one's person to the other. This total self-giving, as spiritual-corporeal as the partners themselves, is the communication of new life, not only in the sense indicated above as the mutual enrichment of the partners, but also in the concrete sense that a new human person is conceived and born into this world. It is the highest expression of their mutual love, one which becomes concrete as the presence of a new person, different from the parents but,

still, totally coming forth from their action of love. Not without reason is this seen as a special participation in, or cooperation with the love of the Creator, who made man the visible expression of His loving goodness.

3. The child which has been born is not destined solely to be the concrete result of the human love of the parents. Just as the parents find their ultimate dignity in making God's kindness and love visible on earth, so does their child have the same destiny. Just as the parents reach their salvation and redemption by making their life the expression of God's love within the human society, so also must the child find his ultimate perfection, salvation and redemption by his personal dedication to God in his own responsible activity on earth. The development of these qualities is an essential and inseparable part of the human procreation. It is the exalted dignity of human fruitfulness not only to transmit human life, but also to guide and to protect this life until it is able to assume its personal responsibility before God, and thus achieves redemption.

These three aspects of human fruitfulness are so completely interwoven in our human reality that one cannot even be adequately thought of without including the others. On the other hand, because of our human limitations, the individual couple can hardly ever give concrete and full expression to this fruitfulness. It is the task of the human couple to find a balance in their expression of it. In the search for this balance they should realize that there are two extremes, namely, "under-fruitfulness" and "over-fruitfulness." Let me explain what I mean.

By "under-fruitfulness" I want to convey that a couple could be selfish in their mutual self-giving. Their marital state does not grow to a maturity in which the other person is the primary concern of *either* partner. I stress *either* because this responsibility rests equally upon both. The consequences are many. Their mutual fulfillment and growth suffers proportionately to the degree of their self-orientation, or to the extent of their search for self-gratification. This may result in limiting the number of children to the level which "pleases" them, not to the level which is "better" for them. This self-oriented attitude is, whether verbalized or not, conveyed to their children who will somehow be adversely affected by it.

By "over-fruitfulness" I mean the attitude that one should give birth to as many children as is physically possible, regardless of whether or not the couple is able to take care of their further development which is so much a part of the procreative task. The usual justification for this attitude is that every child is a gift of God and that it must be received as such.

In itself it sounds good and praiseworthy to leave the regulation and size of the family to "God's providence." It is possible, however, that by saying this a couple overlooks an important aspect, namely, that God's providence expresses itself not only in biological laws but, also, and specifically for man, by using his intellect. The Creator gave man not only existence, but also a share in the shaping of his existence. In the circumstances of their own lives the couple is able to a certain extent to recognize what God's service demands of them; and they must contribute to the achievement of this goal to the best of their abilities. It is not at all impossible, especially at the present time, that unrestricted "generative fruitfulness" may prove to be a severe handicap and an obstacle to the fulfillment of the total task of marriage. It is the special task of the married couple to find the balance in their own life, a balance which is so delicate that no one can ever describe it with any degree of exactitude.

Only the couple themselves may be able to come to a decision about the size of their family. As Vatican Council says:

> The parents themselves and no one else should ultimately make this judgment in the sight of God (*The Church in the Modern World,* No. 50).

Since the whole existence of the partners is so deeply immeshed in marriage and family with their mutual relationship and with their relationship to God, it is clear that this specific aspect is a serious responsibility in conscience.

2. Fruitfulness and Family Size

Not without reason does our age speak about the virtue of responsible parenthood, because in this particular decision a large number of responsibilities of the parents' lives fuse together into one great expression of love for the Creator, which is made visible in the generous and conscientious approach to their specific task in life. The Vatican Council points out that procreation does not only mean the "transmission of human life, but also the education of those to whom human life has been transmitted." When we speak of education, we have again a concept which cannot be accurately described. Too many factors are involved, such as the child's intellectual abilities, the social demands of the present time in general and of the parents in particular, the interest of the child, etc.

What the Council seems to point out is that together with human life the "human values of life" also must be transmitted as far as this is possible, given the capacities and circumstances of the couple. The task of the parents continues until the child is, in normal human estimation, capable of setting his own course of life and assuming personal responsibility before God and society. It seems obvious that in this matter no exact calculations can be made either concerning the number of children which a couple can raise, or concerning the quality and the degree of education which they should receive. The conscientious decision of the couple will be ultimately decisive.

There is difficulty in finding a basis for this decision. The Vatican Council presents a number of factors which should be taken into account:

> Let them thoughtfully take into account both their own welfare and that of their children, those already born and those which the future may bring. For this accounting they need to reckon with both the material and the spiritual conditions of the times as well as of their state in life. Finally, they should consult the interests of the family group, of temporal society, and of the Church herself (*Ibid.*, No. 50).

This text gives a description of the whole human arrangement of the family as it exists in the society in which we are living. The couples are reminded that human dignity is not plain existence, but that it demands a condition and development which is reasonably in accordance with the cultural development of our time and place. It must take into account contemporary demands of intellectual development and of religious education. The first consideration is the present number of children, and as far as human projection can go, the couples must consider what the chances and possibilities are for those who might still be born.

An absolute certainty and security can never be given. In every aspect of life man takes risks, therefore, also in this aspect man should have the courage to take risks which are reasonable, and they should be guided by courageous generosity rather than fearfulness. In many cases one or another of the indicated circumstances will advise a limitation of the family. In other cases it will be the combination of several or all circumstances which present themselves to the decision of the couple. Many will feel insecure and doubtful about the course which is to be taken with regard to the spacing of the children or with regard to the number of children they can take care of responsibly. To seek advice is always a very wise thing, but the ultimate decision before God will rest upon their own shoulders.

Assuming that, in a generous decision before God, the couple decide that either a spacing of the children or a temporary or permanent halt is necessary, then they will be faced with the problem of how this spacing or a complete halt can be achieved. They will be confronted simultaneously with two responsibilities, both of which are very serious matters of conscience. Their marital responsibilities to each other, to their family, and to God demand that no child be conceived at this time, but the same marital responsibilities demand just as seriously that their conjugal love should continue to ripen and grow. This continuation of conjugal love still demands the expression of the whole human person in each partner.

They know that there are many ways in which they can show to each other their deep respect and love. None of these is deeper than conjugal intimacy, but they know also that the full expression of conjugal intimacy includes the possibility of a new conception, for which precisely at this juncture they cannot accept responsibility before God.

Such situations can place a couple in a serious dilemma. On the one hand, they see it as an injustice, perhaps even as a serious injustice, toward their marriage and their family if the number of children is increased at this moment. In certain cases it can even seem to them as a serious sin before God to expand voluntarily the family which they already have. On the other hand, they feel that in their circumstances a prolonged abstinence from conjugal intimacy would jeopardize the very existence of their marriage, despite all generosity and prayerful efforts. To endanger their marriage and the education of their children to such an extent may seem to them a serious sin before God as well. Not always will the situation be so problematic that they feel themselves facing a "serious" sin whatever way they turn, but basically it is this collision of responsibilities which is the heart of the problem. In this connection we must once again insist on the importance of conjugal intimacy in married life. About the specific marital acts of intimacy the Vatican Council says:

> The actions within marriage by which the couple are united intimately and chastely are noble and worthy ones. Expressed in a manner

which is truly human, these actions promote the
mutual self-giving by which the spouses enrich
each other with a joyful and ready will (*The
Church in the Modern World,* No. 49).

However physical the actions may superficially
seem to be, in their deepest reality they are the
most personal self-giving of the one partner to the
other. They result in a fulfillment and gratification
of the partners which certainly is physical, but in
and through the physical aspects it reaches the
depth of the personalities which are enriched in
the experience of the self-giving of the spouses.
These actions are one of the ways in which the
spouses grow to greater personal maturity. In this
sense these actions, even apart from generation,
have in themselves an element of fruitfulness in so
far that they produce this development and
growth in each other. It is a reassurance of gratitude for the past and a guarantee of unity for the
future.

But this benefit for the spouses themselves is
not the only reason why this intimacy can remain
a necessity for many couples, even at times when
no new life may be transmitted. Let us again take
first the Church's teaching on this point:

Where the intimacy of married life is broken
off, its faithfulness can sometimes be imperiled
and its quality of fruitfulness be ruined, for then
the upbringing of the children and the courage to

accept new ones are both endangered (*Ibid.,* No. 51).

The Council gives in this text the plain psychological fact that for the unity of the couple and for their mutual cooperation in the upbringing of the family the most intimate union between the partners is an almost essential requirement. But a good look at the text tells us even more. When the Council says that the faithfulness may be imperiled if these intimate relations are broken off, it recognizes the same human condition about which St. Paul wrote to his Christians in Corinth:

> Do not deprive each other, except perhaps by consent, for a time, that you may give yourselves to prayer; and return together again lest Satan tempt you because you lack self-control (1 Cor. 7:5).

It is a plain human fact that man and woman have an urge for each other which pulls them together. This same urge, which is the ultimate basis for their mutual love, could become the source of their separation because of human weakness. As with every condition of human existence, marital love needs to be protected if it is to remain stable, to grow and ripen.

But there is more. The upbringing of the children, their education and the development of their personality is seen as most intimately connected with the mutual relationship between the spouses. This is an aspect or rather a special quality of human fruitfulness. This, too, is the transmission of life, but now specified in terms of human values. The respect which the children will have for themselves; the respect and joy which they will develop for their own "being a boy" or "being a girl" will to a considerable degree depend on the balanced attitude of the parents. The respect which each of the children will develop for the "other sex" is in no small degree based upon the respect which they witness in the mutual relationship of their parents. Therefore, in marriage as a human reality and as a relationship to God, the conjugal intimacy, even when no new conception may follow, is still in a very real sense an expression of "love which by its nature is fruitful." Perhaps we may even go so far as to say that the correctly understood fruitfulness in marriage demands that at certain times the couple need to enjoy conjugal intimacy *from which new conception is positively and effectively excluded,* because otherwise the total fruitfulness itself would be seriously endangered.

It is obvious that at this point the moral problems may become difficult. One might say that it is easy enough to prevent conception. The present stage of development in medical science offers many possibilities. This is certainly true, but not less important is the question whether the possibilities which medical science offers are morally acceptable. What medicine offers is immediately directed toward the biological process. However, the biological process is an integral part of the human being and thus of marriage. If marriage, and specifically the conjugal intimacy, is a *total* self-giving of one partner to the other, then this totality must include a deep respect for the other partner as he or she is, and no exception should be made with regard to the biological aspects nor with regard to any other aspects.

Any infringement or willful limitation of any of the human aspects would constitute an infringement on the totality of the persons, and thus on the totality of the self-giving in marriage. This "falling short" of the totality would already occur if marriage is considered merely as a human institution, but it becomes still more objectionable if we consider the sacramental meaning of marriage. In the sacramental meaning marriage is intended to be the living human expression and human sign which is the reality of the redemptive and total self-giving of Christ to the Church and, at the same time, the reality of the Church's response to Christ. The sacramental aspect, therefore, does not change the human reality but it strengthens it and gives it a deeper meaning.

Since the human reality and the sacramental meaning totally coincide, it will be good first to examine what the Church's teaching is on this subject. Vatican Council II says:

> The sexual characteristics of man and the human faculty of reproduction wonderfully exceed the dispositions of lower forms of life (*Ibid.*, No. 51).

This is the reason why these human expressions must be honored with great reverence. They may not be considered nor may they be treated as mere biochemical functions. It also means that man is not subject to these biochemical laws in the same way as animals are subject to them. They impose upon man a moral responsibility. This would appear to mean that man is responsible for their correct functioning with relation to the totality of marriage. Concerning the way in which this responsibility is to be approached the Council says:

> When there is a question of harmonizing conjugal love with the responsible transmission of life, the moral aspect of any procedure does not depend solely on sincere intentions or on evaluation of motives, but must be determined by objective standards. These, based on the nature of the human person and his acts preserve the full sense of mutal self-giving and human procreation in the context of conjugal love. Such a goal cannot be achieved unless the virtue of conjugal chastity is sincerely practiced.

> Relying on these principles, sons of the Church may not undertake methods of birth control which are found blameworthy by the teaching authority of the Church in its unfolding of the divine law (*Ibid.,* No. 51).

This text of the Council speaks only about the prevention of conception. Earlier in the same document the Council had positively rejected every effort to destroy fetal life for the purpose of family limitation. It is interesting to note that in the discussion of methods for the prevention of new conception, the Council does not speak about any specific methods. This specification the Pope explicitly reserved to himself. He would give an answer after serious study by a special commission. The Council text itself, however, provided the basis upon which this further elaboration was to be built. Four important points are given in this text:

1. A sincere subjective intention and evaluation of motives is by itself not sufficient to make a moral decision on any method.

2. The moral decision must be determined by *objective* standards which are based upon human dignity and take into account all the aspects of marriage (fruitful love).

3. To reach this high goal it is necessary to practice conjugal chastity.

4. The guidelines of the teaching authority of the Church should be followed.

3. The Human Person as Objective Standard of Morality

In this Council text it is noteworthy that the human person is taken as the basic and objective standard. The words "human person and his acts" refer to man in all his human relationships. It includes the human intentions, the expression of self-giving and fruitfulness. It also points to the God-relatedness of man where it mentions the practice of chastity and respect for teaching authority. By making the totality of the human being so explicitly the basis for future decision, the Council indicates that it refuses to grade the various values existing in the human person. Man's task will be to preserve the totality as far as this is possible in a human approach.

This point is very important because in the teachings of Pope Pius XI and Pius XII any infringement at the biological level (other than rhythm) which was not evidently and exclusively a medical action, was branded as in itself a mortal sin, while little, if anything, was said about other aspects which are also inseparably inherent to marriage. The frequent need to re-iterate this point indicates very clearly that this papal standpoint was never quietly accepted by the Church at large. During the Council there emerged a relatively strong tendency to deny that the biological structures are so important that they should never be over-ruled by other considerations.

When, then, finally the Council decided to consider the "human dignity and totality of marriage" as the ultimate basis, and left to the Pope the final decision with regard to the use of various individual methods, the Council had at least given the assurance that the overriding importance of man's biological structure was not an aspect which should, by itself, be placed in opposition to all the other values taken together. Whatever in the future its place would be, the biological structure could not be considered independently from the conjugal totality without violating the Council's teaching. Though the Council did not speak infallibly, it cannot be disregarded by anyone.

4. The Encyclical "On Human Life"

After a long period of study, prayer and reflection, Pope Paul VI finally issued the encyclical ON HUMAN LIFE as the answer to the question which he had reserved for himself. With regard to the integrity of the biological functions in the conjugal relationship, the Pope repeats first the absolute disapproval of the destruction of fetal life, as the Council had done earlier. He adds to it the disapproval of sterilization either in male or female, and finally with regard to the methods which were under discussion before, during and after the Council, he says:

> Similarly excluded is every action which, either in anticipation of the conjugal act, or in its accomplishment, or in the development of its natural consequences, proposes, whether as an end or as a means, to render procreation impossible (No. 14).

From the context it is very clear that the Pope refers to all chemical and mechanical means which by their nature interfere with the biological generative process. Even the word procreation is used here in a purely biological sense. With regard to the chemical means, he only makes an exception for "the use of those therapeutic means truly necessary to cure diseases of the organism" (No. 15). The only way which the encyclical indicates as licit for the regulation of conception is rhythm.

If we read the parts of the encyclical which speak about the ways of regulating conception (Nos. 13–18) by themselves, they are very disturbing. One gets the feeling that developments in science and new ways of thinking have been completely ignored and that the development of theological thinking has been pushed back approximately fifty years. The Pope based his arguments on the demands of "natural law," but he seems to understand the concept of natural law exclusively in the sense of biological laws of nature. This particular concept of natural law was prevalent during the last centuries and was based upon a misinterpretation of Aquinas and Augustine, but during the last few decades this concept has been almost entirely relinquished. Even Vatican Council II—which includes Pope Paul—seems to take issue with it when it says:

> The sexual characteristics of man and the human faculty of reproduction wonderfully exceed the disposition of lower forms of life (*The Church in the Modern World*, No. 51).

Further, he makes a comparison between the biological order and other values in marriage when he says that the biological structures may

not be violated even if it is to "safeguard, or promote individual, family or social well-being (No.
14). Thus, he seems to place the biological structures again as an independent value over and
against the totality of marriage. This seems to
bring theology back to *Casti Connubii*, but
exactly this approach was not accepted by the
Council—and this includes Pope Paul. Other ex-
amples of apparent contradiction between the encyclical and the last Council could be given, but
these two are sufficient to show why the reading of
this specific part of the encyclical is disturbing.

However, it would be an injustice to the Pope
and to the encyclical to take this part out of context, and it would equally be an injustice to take
the whole encyclical out of context, and this
means not to make a serious effort to interpret it
in the light of the Vatican Council. Looking at the
encyclical in its totality, we can see (apart from
the introduction) three major parts: First, the
total vision of man and in this light a vision on the
totality of marriage and the re-affirmation that
the conjugal act is by its nature "unitive and procreative" as one inseparable unit. Secondly, and
this we must see in the light of the foregoing, the
indication of illicit and licit means of regulation of
conception. And, finally, we have the pastoral
directives.

The first part on the total vision of man can
with relative ease be connected with the teaching
of Vatican Council II, as this is given in the *Pasto-*

ral Constitution on the Church in the Modern World, Part Two, Chapter One. This suffices to warn us of the Pope's intentions. He wants us to see what he will say next in the specific light of this view of human dignity and totality. In this light the Pope says in the second part that any infringement on the biological level militates against the totality of marriage as the Council has willed it. We may feel unhappy with the way in which it has been expressed, and specifically about the absoluteness which the biological aspects seem to take, but the repeated stress which the Pope places on his concern for the integrity and holiness of marriage does not allow us to see this part independently from this totality. The only conclusion, then, which I can see at this moment is that the Pope stresses the biological so strongly in order to counteract opinions which seem to underrate its importance. He seems to stress that the biological is as much a part of the human totality as any other aspect and, therefore, the consideration of other aspects (individual, family and social) may not be used to outweigh the biological.

As to the question how serious a transgression of the biological order would it be, the Pope does not give an answer. However, in the third part he demands the utmost reverence for the integrity and holiness of marriage, and urges a display of great leniency and understanding on the part of the pastors when they meet with people who are of good-will but who cannot as yet live up to the high

ideal which the encyclical seems to ask. What this
means with regard to moral responsibility will be
discussed later. The most important point is that
we understand clearly that the Pope here again
stresses the totality of marriage as a human reality
and as a sacrament. This means also that Pope
Paul's approach differs widely from that of Pius
XI and Pius XII who considered only this biological aspect and branded a transgression of it as
"mortal" sin. In this encyclical the biological aspect has been maintained as an integral aspect of
marriage, but its "independent absoluteness" has
disappeared.

Earlier I quoted the text of Vatican Council II
which says that the harmonizing of conjugal love
with the responsible transmission of life cannot be
achieved unless the virtue of conjugal chastity is
sincerely practiced. This seems to me to be very
important. Virtue as a general concept may be
described as a condition in which one fulfills with
a certain facility and with a certain degree of success one's human responsibilities in relation to
God. If we narrow this down to a particular area
of life, for our purpose here, the sexual interhuman relationship, then we speak about the virtue
of chastity. This, again, we can consider in general
terms as the habit by which we, with a certain
degree of success, fulfill our human responsibilities with regard to our being man or woman, indi-
vidually as well as in relation to the other sex.

In the full human context this will mean that we

respect our own sexuality and use it according to our state of life, including of course the circumstances of our life. It refers to external behavior as well as to internal tendencies. Chastity has, therefore, nothing negative about it, but it is the positive approach to life. In our total interhuman relationship we are man or woman. As such we must respect ourselves and relate to others.

In the context of marriage the man-woman relationship has its own particular meaning and expression, and chastity in marriage must express this specific interpersonal relationship. It includes the whole personality just as marriage itself includes the whole personality. Chastity is specifically related to the sexual relationship. This means it refers to the bodily expression and unity of love between the spouses. This specific conjugal relationship and intimacy is a total giving of the one to the other in bodily expression as a concrete realization of their love for each other. Consequently, we must say that their mutual expression is chaste whenever it belongs to this expression of total self-giving.

The individual pleasure, including the physical pleasure, of each of the partners, as well as the pleasure which they give to each other share in the goodness and in the chastity of the act of intimacy. But whenever the pleasure seeking becomes selfish and when the primary reason for the bodily expression is self-gratification, then the conjugal intimacy itself is no longer the full expression of *mutual* love, and to the same degree the virtue of chastity is violated. We should not misunderstand this. Circumstances of life, the urge and needs of the human being, man as well as woman, can make a person feel a strong attraction to his or her partner. This cannot be considered as selfish. This specific attraction and need is one of the ways in which the Creator has structured the mutual needs and the mutual fulfillments of man and woman. Both should react to the needs of the other. But when this urge demands satisfaction at the expense of respect for the other partner, no matter for what reason, then it becomes a self-seeking, because one partner does not take into account the other's needs.

Repeatedly it has been stressed that the partners' self-giving must be total; this means, that it must include all human aspects, biological as well as psychological, social, etc. This applies also to the expression of conjugal chastity. This expression must take into account all these various aspects of conjugal love. We may even say that, with regard to the "sexual" relationship in marriage, conjugal love and conjugal chastity coincide. Both refer to the deeply human and total self-giving of the one to the other. The term "conjugal chastity" stresses that this total self-giving contains an explicit reference to the Creator.

The encyclical *On Human Life* also speaks about conjugal chastity, but it uses the unfortunate expression "mastery of self." This might give the impression of negativism, as if one looks down upon the man-woman relationship in its deepest mutual surrender. However, despite this approach, which sounds more like Stoicism than Christian virtue, I still think that the encyclical refers to the same reality of conjugal chastity. There can be no doubt that respect for the other partner will impose a certain self-restraint on a person, but this self-restraint is part of the expression of total marital love and respect. Where the full expression of conjugal intimacy may not be or cannot be obtained at a certain moment, mutual love must still find expression in physical ways which are good and chaste.

It is this development and growth of conjugal chastity to which the Vatican Council refers and which it regards as necessary for achieving harmony between the expression of conjugal love and the transmission of human life. As every virtue, conjugal chastity also is a matter of growth and, therefore, it has its hardships throughout its stages of development. Just as it is not always easy to grow in patience and helpfulness for others, so the growth in conjugal chastity will continuously demand a certain degree of restraint. But this self-restraint itself is not less the expression of love for the partner. It is a special expression of the fruitfulness which is intrinsically inherent in conjugal love.

Chapter Six

THE SEARCH FOR A
RESPONSIBLE ANSWER

If the foregoing pages have given the impression that this whole book aims at giving an answer to the question of the regulation of conception, then they are largely misunderstood. What I wanted to give above everything else was an explanation of the meaning of marriage and its responsibilities. Marriage is not just a function. It is an expression of life. Marriage places its imprint upon the whole human being in all his relationships.

The work in the office or whatever other function the man may have, receives a new dimension by the fact that from the moment he marries, his work is the means to sustain and to support his family. In every important action concerning his job the well-being of his beloved ones is consciously or unconsciously involved in his decision. The woman may have done all sorts of chores in the home of her parents or elsewhere, she may continue to work in the office or hospital, but from the moment she becomes the wife of this husband, all these tasks receive different dimensions and meanings. Marriage encompasses the whole life and existence of the individual partners.

At no stage of our approach have these aspects been excluded. On the contrary, they were positively included. Over and again they have been mentioned, when it was said that marriage has a wide variety of aspects such as biological, psychological, social and others. But at the heart of it all is the love between the partners, a love which is based upon the differentiation of sexes and which from there engulfs their whole personalities. When this love grows and ripens, the meaning of all the other aspects will increase in perspective and depth. When this love ebbs away, the other aspects may either take its place and contribute to a more rapid alienation between the partners, or they may suffer and become meaningless.

1. The Primacy of Conscience and Its Meaning

If, then, at this moment we are searching for a responsible answer with respect to occasions when the expression of love becomes a problem, we are touching the heart of the marriage and the heart of the family life. The basic principles which I propose here for a solution to this specific problem will also be valid for other areas in life, if one can see the principles apart from the particular applications which are made here.

We have discussed how the expression of love

in marriage and responsible transmission of new life can place the couple before a serious dilemma in which each alternative contains a serious obligation in conscience, and might even be seen as a sinful action. In the solution of this problem only one answer can be given, namely, the couple must follow their own conscience. There is nothing radical or new in this statement. This has been the Church's teaching since its origin and it was very clearly restated in Vatican Council II:

> A sense of the dignity of the human person has been impressing itself more and more deeply on the consciousness of contemporary man, and the demand is increasingly made that men should act on their own judgment, enjoying and making use of a responsible freedom, not driven by coercion but motivated by a sense of duty.

> This demand for freedom in the human society chiefly regards the quest for the values proper to the human spirit. The Vatican Council takes careful note of these desires in the mind of men. It proposes to declare them to be greatly in accord with truth and justice (*Declaration on Religious Freedom,* No. 1).

In another document, *The Pastoral Constitution on the Church in the Modern World,* the Council points into the same direction:

> God has willed that man remain 'under the control of his own decisions,' so that he can seek

his Creator spontaneously and come freely to utter and blissful perfection through loyalty to Him. Hence man's dignity demands that he act according to a knowing and free choice that is personally motivated and prompted from within, not under blind internal impulse nor by mere external pressure (No. 16).

This free choice, therefore, though coming from man's interior being, is not the impulse of an instinctual urge, but

> Man has in his heart a law written by God; to obey this law is the very dignity of man; according to this law he will be judged (No. 16).

Here the Council speaks clearly about human conscience which it defines as "the most secret core and sanctuary of man. There he is alone with God, whose voice echoes in his depths" (No. 16).

So great is the power and importance of conscience "that it does not lose its dignity even if it errs from invincible ignorance" (No. 16). God has given to man the faculty of reason by which he must discover in the depth of his heart the laws which God has written, and "every decision of the will which is contrary to the insight of reason, whether this be correct or incorrect, is evil."[1]

Therefore, there can be no doubt that in every human decision the ultimate moral norm for ac-

[1] Thomas Aquinas. *S.T.*, p. I–II, q. 19, a. 5.

tion is the conscience of man. However, there is
hardly anything as difficult to know as what conscience demands. Because in the human being
there is not only the voice of God speaking to
man, but there is also the urge of man's instinctual
drives. To distinguish between these two demands
a profound knowledge of man himself and of his
purpose on earth.

To understand this purpose of human life on
earth there is perhaps no better source than the
teaching of St. Thomas Aquinas. He started his
explanation of the morality of human behavior by
saying that after speaking about God Himself "it
is now our task to consider God's image, that is
man, because he, too, is the source of his own
actions in so far as he has a free will and is the
master of his own activity."[2] While all the other
creatures participate in a certain way in the image
of God because they exist, live or know in a certain way, it is characteristic of man as a rational
creature that he will come to the fulfillment of his
human existence by knowing and loving God.[3]

Elaborating on this point in a later part of his
work, Aquinas goes on to say that everything depends on the will and on the design of God, which
is the eternal law. A creature exists because of the
fact that God has communicated to it an existence; and, therefore, in a certain way the creature
participates in the eternal law, in so far as the

[2] *S.T.*, p. I–II, Prologue.
[3] *S.T.*, p. I–II, q. I, a. 7 c.

creature by the imprint of God's existence has the inclination to perform actions which lead to its fulfillment. But man's participation in the eternal law is much higher, because man "participates in divine providence itself in so far as he is able to take care of himself and of others."[4]

In plain language, this means that man has a special task. He must not merely react to biological and biochemical impulses as other creatures do, but it is his task to share with God in the very planning of his own life. Human life takes shape not only because God has given to man a body with which he lives on earth, but God has also granted to man the faculty of reason, which is the imprint of the divine light in man. With this reason man himself must, as it were, complete his own creation and give a concrete expression to the potentialities which the Creator has given to him.

In this light we can see how the voice of God echoes in the depth of the human heart. It is essential to man that he search in his own existence for the form and the fulfillment which the Creator has placed within the realm of his potentiality. However, because of man's limitations, his weakness and his sinfulness, this voice of God is obscured. Man is earthly despite his heavenly vocation. These two human aspects are so intimately interwoven that during his sojourn on earth man's essential orientation to God comes to him by earthly

[4] *S.T.*, p. I–II, q. 91, a. 2 c.

ways, and his earthly ways are the channels within which he must give expression to the orientation of his life to God. In his developmental process throughout history man in an unending search and with ever greater clarity gradually learns to understand the values of his life. With his own intellect, his greatest gift of God, man "gradually lays bare the laws of society."

In absolute fidelity to the teaching of Thomas Aquinas and of Vatican Council we may say that:

> Human life is a dialogue-in-action between God and man. In this dialogue it is as if the material world and history are placed by God between Him and us as a "translation" of His inner speaking to us. Moreover, history and world are also the means in which and through which man's attention is explicitly drawn to this inner speaking of God, while at the same time this world and history form the environment and the atmosphere within which man can give his response to the task which God has placed upon him.[5]

Seen in this light, the human conscience is not a static reality which absorbs only laws imposed from without, but rather is a continuous self-discovery. Conscience is the gaining of a deeper insight not only into one's own potential, but also into the well-being of others. In his own being man discovers certain things which he either cannot

[5] E. Schillebeeckx, *God en Mens,* Nelissen, 1965, p. 137.

change or which he should not change because he
realizes that by interfering in them, he would destroy or harm his own well-being, the well-being of
others or of society. Here the material world and
historical knowledge of the past become for him
sources of information through which God makes
known to him the design and the orientation of his
life. It is to these directives that man must respond
as best he can according to his particular abilities
and in his particular circumstances. In daily life
God entrusts a task to every human being. This
task does not concern the individual alone, it involves the whole of human society. This task is the
voice of God to man, and in its concrete realization man gives his response to God. His life becomes in a very real sense a dialogue-in-action
between God and himself.

2. Conscience and Freedom

If all this is true, then the human conscience is
as wide as human life itself. To speak of "following one's conscience," thus means that one must
give concrete expression to his life in order to
fulfill his potential with regard to himself, to the
world in which he lives, and to the society of
which he is a member. This is a task in freedom
and in personal responsibility.

The word "freedom" can easily be misunderstood. If we take the concept of freedom to indicate the abstract ability of man to do or not to do
one thing or another, then we might be inclined to

see the concrete expression and the ideal of freedom in the exercise of this ability. Then we would consider ourselves free whenever we can do what pleases us at any moment. This would open the way to complete self-indulgence and to disregard for the well-being of others. But it would ultimately lead to man's self-destruction. If, however, we understand freedom as a moral freedom in which we use the same human abilities and possibilities, but use them for the benefit of the whole of mankind of which the individual knows himself to be a part, then the ultimate result will be proper human development. Moral freedom is the insight that

> Creation has been placed in the hands of man and has been entrusted to his decisions, since it is in the power of man to contribute to its development or to counteract it.[6]

Because of this insight man knows that he has a responsibility which imposes itself upon him as a duty. This duty is not imposed upon him from without, but it is his response to a demand which he feels to be his concern.[7] Responding to this sense of duty, man will continue to labor "to decipher the authentic signs of God's presence and purpose in the happenings, needs and desires of

[6] Gabriel Madinier, De Mens en Zijn Geweten. Spectrum, Utrecht, 1964, p. 77.

[7] cf. Erich Fromm, Man for Himself, Holt, Rinehart and Winston, New York, 1947, p. 99.

mankind."[8] This moral freedom does not exist in following one's instincts, but in freeing oneself from them. It is the mastering of one's instinctual inclinations, of organizing one's life, of building up a spiritual personality and loving what is good.[9]

This conscience and freedom of man is in a state of constant growth. It develops in the interaction of many factors. It is the result of many personal decisions and of deepening knowledge.

> Conscience develops within the society. It is moulded according to the rules and the ideals of the society, and increasingly it interiorizes these rules. But on the other hand the rules and the norms of the society demand an effort on the part of conscience in order to be understood, developed and interpreted. This does not mean that the norms are made by conscience, nor does it mean that conscience is created by the norms of society. Conscience and norms mutually interact.[10]

This seems to make it clear that authority plays an important role in the formation of conscience. It is not as if any authority can ever take over the individual's personal responsibility. Vatican Council says: "God willed that man remain under the control of his own decisions" and "man is not guided by merely external pressure." But this does

[8] *The Church in the Modern World,* No. II.
[9] Madinier, *op. cit.,* p. 80.
[10] Madinier, *op. cit.,* pp. 30–31.

not deny that in the search for the good of the totality, which is so much a part of man's personal search, properly constituted authorities usually are in a better position to discern which actions are contributive to this good. It is their special task to formulate, explain and protect the values of human existence and to outline how these values can best be preserved in particular circumstances of human life. Authority is one of the guidelines which God's wisdom and providence has given to humanity to express His purpose. Therefore, men as sharers in divine providence must use this same means to discover and decipher God's purpose.

It seems obvious that the teaching authority of the Church has in this connection a function which is still more important and still more indispensable. In the Church's teaching authority the guidance of the Spirit of God, which has been given to the Church as a whole, crystallizes and makes this authority in a special way the voice of God speaking to humanity in its search for its purpose and for its moral responsibility.

The teaching authority, however, cannot eliminate the personal responsibility of the individual, because it is God's will that man remain under the control of his own decisions. Man's task, then, would be to listen with great reverence and attention to the voice of this teaching authority and to take its decisions as the starting point for one's search for God's will. One must search in the moral teaching of the Church's magisterium for the depth of the human and God-related values which it tries to explain, and one must see one's life in the light of these values.

It is not impossible that, despite all efforts, someone will not be able to understand the values which the authority has formulated. And it is possible that, in all honesty, the official formulation clashes with one's most sincere convictions. In such circumstances there is only one way left open for the individual conscience, namely, to accept one's own responsibility before God, because God has willed that man remain under the control of his own decisions.

It will be the task of the couple to apply these principles to the formation of their conscience with regard to the important decisions in their conjugal life. Obviously, these principles must enter into every decision concerning their conjugal life, but they have a special importance with regard to their specific conjugal relationship. Evidently the responsible judgment in this matter goes far beyond a personal feeling. Vatican Council reminds us that in the question of harmonizing the expression of conjugal love with the responsible transmission of new life our action must be determined by objective standards which are based on the nature of the human person and his acts, and which preserve the full sense of mutual self-giving and human procreation in the context of conjugal love.

3. Ideal and Reality

This reminder helps us see that it is not a single aspect of human existence which is ultimately decisive, but the human and conjugal totality. The importance of biological structures may not be underestimated, but "man is not wrong when he regards himself as superior to bodily concerns, for in his interior qualities he outstrips the whole sum of mere things."[11] At the same time, however, he must not overlook the purpose of marriage itself which is the living of a conjugal love which by its nature is fruitful. This includes once more all that we have tried to explain in earlier pages. We have tried to convey the full understanding of the fact that by the design of God's creation, man and woman come together to form one principle of cooperation to fulfill the task which the Creator entrusted to them, namely, to continue, shape and complete creation itself. They come together in their mutual attraction based upon the differentiation of the sexes and they unite in an unbreakable bond of love which penetrates their whole being, corporeal as well as spiritual.

This love is the total self-giving of the one to the other in all aspects of their corporeal-spiritual existence, and thus it gives rise to new life, not only in their personal maturation but also in the child that can be born. This human totality, which in its essence has been willed by the Creator as His

[11] *The Church in the Modern World,* No. 14.

image and likeness and as the example of His unreserved self-giving and love for humanity, has become in the economy of salvation the sign and the symbol which not only refers to the redemptive action of Christ, but also is the perceptible expression of this redemptive reality. With this totality as the guiding principle of their life as a couple, the husband and wife face the question of harmonizing the expression of conjugal love with the responsible transmission of new life.

In this view of totality their attention is not primarily drawn to one specific aspect of their conjugal existence. The principal question which pervades their whole scale of values and attitudes should be this one: "How can we express in our actions this sacred commission in all its integrity?" However, at the same time that this question pervades all the dimensions of their marital existence, they also know themselves to be subject to an almost unlimited number of limitations, which stretch from their concrete financial and biological conditions and needs to the more elusive but not less real psychological and spiritual demands.

Thus, the various values inevitably present themselves in a narrow individual fashion and there is a real temptation to trespass on one in order to safeguard another which seems to them more important. It is the mutual incompatibility of various values at the same time at a given period or situation in the life of this specific couple which brings on the difficulties. They know that the ideal totality is at this moment beyond their reach. The total integrity which they want to express cannot be obtained now despite their honesty and generosity. Then this same honesty and generosity make them ask themselves another question: "How can we come as close as possible to this integrity without destroying our marriage itself?" Their primary concern is not the individual values of marriage, but the totality of conjugal life and love with a deep respect for the individual values.

In this judgment their primary concern is to search for that expression which fulfills the law of creation, that the two become one flesh as one source and principle of the fulfillment of God's plan. Inseparably connected with it is the concern to love each other as Christ loved the Church and gave Himself totally and unreservedly for her sanctification. So they, too, want to become, to an ever greater extent, this one source and principle of unreserved mutual self-giving. Its unreservedness consists in giving to each other all they have at this moment of their existence, however little it might be. In this situation the means of regulation of conception have lost their biological significance, they have lost their meaning as methods to find self-gratification. Hedonistic and selfish concerns have been eliminated, and the totality of this conjugal expression becomes an act of love to the Creator and Redeemer expressed in human language. Thus the couple make their own decision before God and their conscience.

4. Again, the Encyclical "On Human Life"

Some may consider the foregoing a poor and unsuccessful attempt to circumvent the explicit statements which are given in the Encyclical ON HUMAN LIFE. Let us try to see clearly what the encyclical does teach. Earlier we have indicated that the encyclical gives much more than a simple prohibition of the use of chemical and mechanical means of regulation of conception. In the document as a whole the emphasis is clearly on the totality of marriage. The text itself says:

> The problem of birth, like every other problem regarding human life, is to be considered, beyond partial perspectives—whether of the biological, psychological, demographic or social orders—in the light of the integral vision of man and of his vocation, not only his natural and earthly, but also his supernatural and eternal vocation (No. 7).

This leaves no doubt that the Pope wants to approach the question of procreation in terms of the totality of marriage both as an earthly reality with all the ramifications which this implies, and as a sacrament in which marriage is the reality of God's sanctifying love in visible human expression. We do not wish to present here a detailed study of the proofs which the encyclical offers to protect the biological values, namely, the prohibition of chemical and mechanical means to prevent conception. But the fact that the whole approach to the subject is placed in the light and in the perspective of this totality should make it clear to us that it is not the Pope's intention to make this one biological aspect of marriage override all other aspects of the human and supernatural meaning of marriage. In the development of the argumentations and proofs—however poorly they may seem to be constructed—we can read very clearly that the Pope wants to stress that the use of such means constitutes an interference with the integrity of the biological order, and therefore also with the integrity of marriage itself. These means as such are "out of order."

What this means for the moral responsibility of the couple should, I hope, be evident now after all that has been said before. To the best of man's abilities these structures must be observed. Any infringement against any of them militates against the integrity of marriage itself. Admittedly the tone and the approach of the encyclical on this specific point sounds harsh and unfeeling. It is the approach of the instructor who in abstract and general terms speaks from an ivory tower about the requirements for the integral expression of an ideal.

It is remarkable how the tone and the flavor of the encyclical change when the encyclical enters into the discussion of the pastoral aspects of the matter. Addressing himself to the couples, the Pope does not mention the matter of artificial means as such. Sure, the encyclical speaks about it, but now in terms of "carrying out their proper vocation even to perfection," and "to be able to achieve the fullness of conjugal life described by the apostle: husbands love your wives as Christ loved the Church." Perhaps the most important aspect of this approach is formulated as follows:

> And if sin should still keep its hold over them, let them not be discouraged, but rather have recourse with perseverance to the mercy of God, which is poured forth in the sarcrament of penance (No. 25).

Let the word "sin" which is used here—the only time in the whole encyclical—not deter anyone. For lack of a better word, this term is used in moral theology to express any shortcoming which might range from a material defect which is not at all under human responsibility (so-called material sin) to the willful rejection of God (formal sin). The encyclical does in no way make any judgment about the degree of sinfulness. It only points to the falling short of the ideal reality, while the degree of sinfulness is known only to man in the depth of his heart where he is alone with God. No word of condemnation is heard; on the contrary, a supporting hand is held out to those who seek perfection.

The encyclical addresses itself in a tone of heartfelt concern not only to the couples but also to the priests who are the immediate pastors concerned with the spiritual well-being of all. The Pope says that he turns to them with confidence. Confidence in what?

> Your first task—especially in the case of those who teach moral theology—is to expound the Church's teaching on marriage without ambiguity (No. 28).

Here again the understanding of marriage in its totality is the first and foremost concern of the Pope. But in this teaching let the pastors not forget that life is not always easy and that sacrifices can be demanded. All of this, however, must be seen in the overall and total picture of marriage. Within this totality the priest must display an understanding and openness for the complications and difficulties of marriage, to such an extent that

> married couples may always find, in the words and in the heart of the priest, the echo of the voice and the love of the Redeemer (No. 29).

At the same time, it is his task to help them to understand the full meaning of married life in its sacramental dimension. And where this fullness of expression cannot yet be obtained at this moment the priest should

THE SEARCH FOR AN ANSWER

prepare them to recourse often and with faith to the sacraments of the Eucharist and Penance and never to allow themselves to be discouraged at their own weakness (No. 29).

Add to this the Pope's explicit appeal to the bishops whose task, he says, is

to work ardently and incessantly for the safeguarding and the holiness of marriage, so that it may always be lived in its entire human and Christian fulness (No. 30).

The stress falls again upon the entire human and Christian fullness of marriage which is the commission of the married couple. This fullness is the goal which is to be achieved to the best of the couple's ability. Here we come again to the same conclusion which we have drawn before, namely, that it is the task of this couple to search how they can achieve, in serious generosity, that form of perfection which is closest to their possibilities in the *full* expression of marital love.

Here again it can happen that at a certain moment in the life of the couple the marital expression in its full totality is beyond their reach, while at the same time conjugal intimacy seems to them an absolute necessity in honest conscience. Both generative fruitfulness and abstention appear to them as sinful before God. They may feel obliged to use some kind of means. They know that this militates against a certain aspect of the total marital expression. They understand that chemical and mechanical means always militate against a certain aspect of conjugal totality, while rhythm does not always militate against it, and they will try in every available way to develop the ability to live according to this understanding. But they know also that rhythm, though it may protect the biological structures, may damage the psychological aspects and thus jeopardize the marriage as a whole. This would prevent them from living the entire human Christian fullness of marriage for which the encyclical asks. Then before God they must make a decision.

As objective standards in making a judgment about the moral evaluation of the conjugal relationship the Council indicates "the nature of the human person and his acts which must preserve the full sense of mutual self-giving and human procreation in the context of conjugal love" (*The Church in the Modern World*, No. 51). When this text was under discussion in the preparatory stages a proposal was made which was not inserted into the text in order to keep the text as brief as possible, but it was noted and preserved as an explanation of the correct meaning of the moral guideline which the text gives. This explanation says:

Every action which, in a spirit of generosity, harmoniously respects human integrity is morally acceptable. An act contains human integrity when it harmoniously merges all the physical, psychological and moral components of conjugal life into a totality. Not a single element may be excluded, but the function of every element depends on the question whether it is an objectively necessary contribution to make marriage a marriage.[12]

The total integrity of marriage with all its human values comes always to the foreground as the basis upon which the couple must make its decision. Without minimizing the importance of any aspect the couple must allow their decisions to be guided by this conjugal love which by its nature is fruitful.

If one gives biological functioning over-riding importance, then it is forgotten that human existence outstrips the whole sum of mere things. We should remember that marriage, by the will of the Creator, should be guided by the love of man and woman and that in this love all other aspects must obtain their fulfillment in a process of continuous growth. Then the couple should be able to see how amid human limitations and weaknesses and despite human failures and only partial successes, they can live this high ideal of being the visible

[12] Van Heylen, "De Waardigheid van Huwelijk en Gezin," *De Kerk in de Wereld van Deze Tijd,* Paul Brand, 1967, p. 144.

reality of the sanctifying and redemptive action of the Creator and Redeemer. They should much less reflect upon their own limitations than in gratitude to God make a continuous effort to let their lives be in perceptible form

THE LOVE OF GOD IN HUMAN LANGUAGE.